PRAISE FOR
MONSTERS, MARTYRS, AND MARIONETTES:
ESSAYS ON MOTHERHOOD

"In this stunning and deeply personal collection of essays, Adrienne Gruber explores modern motherhood in all its beautiful, terrifying, confusing, grotesque, joyful, sometimes mundane, sometimes ridiculous glory, in a way that is both intimate and yet wholly universal. With a poet's ear for language—unsentimental, startling, sharp as a razor—and a memoirist's knack for finding meaning in the chaotic churn of everyday life, Gruber cracks open her own heart to show you the truth in your own. Honest, tender, and firmly rooted in the body and its connection to the natural world, *Monsters, Martyrs, and Marionettes* is a deep, anguished howl in the dark, a love letter to a complex family, and a careful catalogue of the things we pass on, and the things we must carry on our own."

—AMY JONES, AUTHOR OF *PEBBLE & DOVE*

"The essays in this book, like Gruber's articulation of the chimera, reveal a matrilineal narrative of split flesh, eyeballs, sour milk, creepy puppets, blood, illnesses, and grief that leave the nerves exposed. Gruber writes with the precision of a scalpel, revealing with great dexterity, care, and fierceness a beast that lives across lives and stories."

—ELIZABETH ROSS ROSS, AUTHOR OF *AFTER BIRTH*

MONSTERS, MARTYRS, AND MARIONETTES

ESSAYS ON MOTHERHOOD

ADRIENNE GRUBER

ESSAIS NO. 16

Book*hug Press
Toronto 2024

Library and Archives Canada Cataloguing in Publication

Title: Monsters, martyrs, and marionettes : essays on motherhood /
Adrienne Gruber. Names: Gruber, Adrienne, 1980- author.
Series: Essais (Toronto, Ont.) ; no. 16.
Description: Series statement: Essais series ; no. 16
Identifiers: Canadiana (print) 20230560733 | Canadiana (ebook) 20230560768
ISBN 9781771669030 (softcover)
ISBN 9781771668965 (EPUB)
Subjects: LCSH: Motherhood. | LCGFT: Essays.
Classification: LCC PS8613.R79 M66 2024 | DDC C814/.6—dc23

The production of this book was made possible through the generous
assistance of the Canada Council for the Arts and the Ontario Arts Council.
Book*hug Press also acknowledges the support of the Government of Canada
through the Canada Book Fund and the Government of Ontario through
the Ontario Book Publishing Tax Credit and the Ontario Book Fund.

Book*hug Press acknowledges that the land on which we operate is the
traditional territory of many nations, including the Mississaugas of the Credit,
the Anishnabeg, the Chippewa, the Haudenosaunee, and the Wendat peoples. We
recognize the enduring presence of many diverse First Nations, Inuit, and Métis
peoples, and are grateful for the opportunity to meet and work on this territory.

For Tamsin Martha Clare MacKenzie Hill

CONTENTS

Prologue: Other Mother 9

MONSTERS
Catalogue *19*
Hunger: Notes to My Middle Daughter *25*
Erosion *33*
Fractal *46*

MARTYRS
I Let Out My Breath *55*
The Smell of Screaming *65*
Blood Month *73*
A Route That Does Not Include Your Child *103*

MARIONETTES
Chimera *117*
How She Runs *137*
Vigil for the Vigilant *141*
You're Wrong About *155*

Notes *166*
Acknowledgements *168*
About the Author *171*

Prologue: Other Mother

It's my turn to pick the movie for our family movie night. I've chosen *Coraline*, a stop-motion animation about an only child who finds a small brick door in the house her family has recently moved into. It turns out this brick door is a portal to another dimension, a home identical to her own. One afternoon, Coraline crawls through the portal into an identical kitchen and sees another mother who looks just like her real mother but has buttons sewn, criss-crossed, over her eyes.

Visually the movie is stunning. The richly textured scenery is riveting for my two older daughters, Quintana, eight, and Tamsin, five. Dagney, the baby, doesn't know what she's looking at, but she babbles at the screen, inserting herself into the dialogue so as not to be left out.

In the alternate dimension, Coraline's parents are everything her actual parents aren't—attentive, engaging, doting. They make Coraline extravagant meals, play games with her, and give her love in ways they don't in her day-to-day life.

There's just one small catch—Other Mother wants to steal Coraline's eyes and sew buttons onto her eye sockets.

I've started making pizza from scratch for our movie nights because my eight-year-old refuses to eat pizza from Nat's Pizzeria, our usual go-to takeout place. Mothering seems to mean screwing oneself over for the sake of your kids. Mothering is a concept somebody made up. Mothering moments are made up of tasks and those tasks go unnoticed and unacknowledged and remain unseen.

After we watch the movie, Quintana starts calling me Other Mother. She runs away from me as I chase her with a toothbrush at bedtime, begging me not to sew buttons over her eyes. She cackles as I cringe. Matrilineal lines have blurred since her birth. I'm not sure which mother I am.

MONSTERS

At the Vancouver Aquarium, two-year-old Quintana and I wander past rays, cuttlefish, and a goliath grouper. The darkened tunnels in the exhibit are like an ominous ocean. Navy lighting moves in mock waves along the floor. We come across a taxidermized female shark. Her open cavity presents three fetal sharks inside, while three plasticized baby sharks swim alongside her. Partially digested shrimp and the ringlet tentacles of a former squid are rigid in her intestine. Her skin is sickly beige. The babies in her womb are fully formed; tiny teeth jut out of their open mouths like arrowheads.

This new exhibit is modelled after the popular decades-old "Bodies" exhibit, where real human cadavers were preserved in a revolutionary polymer preservation technique. Plastics, like silicone rubber, polyester, or epoxy resin, replace water and fatty material from dissected bodies. At the aquarium, obscure fish and other aquatic creatures are similarly presented; the cadavers showcase fully circulating arteries and veins, nervous systems, muscles, and sinewy tendons.

Just as Quintana reaches out to poke a fetal shark, a volunteer approaches and asks if I'm familiar with the cannibalization of shark embryos. I stare at him for a moment, trying to register why he's asking me this while also noting the eager grin on his face. He informs me that when shark embryos have different fathers, one dominant fetal shark will grow larger and stronger by devouring the others. Sometimes two will share in the devouring, but only two who share the same father. It's a kind of strategic competition in which the males try to ensure their paternity. The strongest, quickest growing embryo is ultimately the one that secures patrilineality.

"What do you think about that?" the volunteer asks, his eyes shifting from my swollen belly to my face. I shrug and smile politely. Quintana yanks my hand and pulls me into another darkened room with various prehistoric-looking creatures. She runs up to one and touches it and another volunteer glares at me. There are DO NOT TOUCH signs everywhere. When I attempt to restrain her, she throws her head back and shrieks.

Just like sharks, human fetuses can perform these gruesome cannibalistic acts. Vanishing twin syndrome occurs when the fetal tissue is either absorbed by the other twin or by the mother herself. In most cases the healthy fetus waits until the non-viable one dies before absorbing it, but sometimes a partially developed fetus becomes incorporated into a normally developing one. This is called fetus in fetu. There are articles on this phenomenon, one with the title "Baby Born Pregnant With Her Own 'Twins'!" reporting that an infant in Hong Kong was born with an unidentifiable mass that turned out to be two fetuses, one on her liver and the other on her kidney. Some medical professionals consider these masses to be simple teratomas, tumours with tissue and organ components, rather than normally developing fetuses, but many insist they have all the cellular makeup of a potential human.

Years ago, I had emergency surgery in New Mexico to remove a thirteen-centimetre teratoma attached to my left ovary. The surgeon showed me a picture of the mass, tangles of hair like seagrass wrapped around it. She had to remove part of the ovary where the mass was stuck. "Don't worry," she said during pre-op, "your right ovary will still work perfectly." It did, and a few years later I found myself pregnant with my first daughter.

While thrilled to be pregnant, I was immediately anxious about the idea of giving birth. To curb this paralyzing fear, my husband Dennis and I registered for Hypnobabies, a special prenatal class with six regimented sessions that focused on using hypnosis in childbirth to manage and potentially transcend pain.

There were six couples in the class. At the first session, we were instructed to shield ourselves from negative stories and media dramatizations of birth with what the instructor called our bubble of peace. We would close our eyes and visualize being enveloped in a translucent sheath where only positive messages of birth could penetrate. We could welcome anyone into our bubble so long as they were fully supportive of our birth plan and the Hypnobabies ideology. Dennis was in my bubble, along with our futon where we watched TV every night, a plate of chocolate chip cookies, and our three-legged cat, Grendel. Sometimes my mom was there, depending on how on board she was with this method.

Included in the Hypnobabies philosophy was a complete change in the language of birth. Instead of saying labour, we said *birthing time*. Pain became *pressure*. Contractions were waves or surges.

"Language can severely impact your birthing experience," our instructor warned us. "It's important to use positive self-talk when referring to your birthing time."

There was homework every night—meditation CDs to listen to, pregnancy and birth affirmations to repeat, and activities to do with your birth partner intended to encourage deeper intimacy and bonding with the baby. (Not a fetus. Never a fetus). Every night, I'd lie down on the bed with Grendel and close my eyes, listening to the woman's bewitching voice instructing me to count backward from three and transform myself into a state of complete relaxation.

Regardless of this preparation, as the weeks passed and my due date (or in Hypnobabies speak, *guess date*) approached, my dread loomed.

Ancient navigators thought the sea was filled with a number of dangerous sea monsters, but the Kraken, a legendary cephalopod-like beast in Nordic folklore was, by far, the most terrifying. So large as to sometimes be mistaken for an island, the danger was not simply the creature itself but the whirlpool left in its wake.

When I gave birth to my daughter, I became the Kraken. Forty hours of unmedicated labour followed by five hours of pushing will do that to a person. I grew extra limbs that flailed and thrashed. With each contraction, I rose from the birth pool like a colossal mollusk, ready to crush and consume.

Pain is meant to be a message to the brain that something's wrong. In birth, pain is indicative of progress, but with that progress, fear barbed itself under my skin. My body's quick recovery from birth proved how effective an unmedicated birth experience could be, but emotionally I felt weak, tortured by the knowledge that I had succeeded in the natural childbirth "dream" and all it did was render me traumatized.

I was shocked when my midwife raised her head from between my legs and declared that I had no tearing. "Are you sure?" I asked, convinced my clitoris had split in two. I couldn't believe there hadn't been permanent damage.

Our apartment mimicked my battered insides. Blood and vomit tinted the water in the birth pool into a murky swamp. Large bloody pads and sheets overflowed from a garbage bag and the carpet was streaked with bright red stains. Grendel had the look of a war casualty, his eyes hollow and dulled from the roaring, exploding woman he witnessed rampaging naked around the apartment for the last two days.

When I told friends and family I had my baby at home, I was met with different reactions. Some expressed relief that I had managed to birth a living and healthy baby without medical assistance, while others considered me a birthing goddess, a warrior. Truthfully, I was a fraud. I couldn't find the empowerment I was promised through Hypnobabies. If only they knew that, after Quintana was born, I wanted to unzip my skin and pull her back inside that space she once inhabited. I resented the trauma it took to release her from my body, and I wanted to consume her the way she consumed me.

My rage often teetered on eruption. Some days I wanted to sink the vessel of obligations she brought into my life. Some days I was swimming in circles, regardless of my wants, and the maelstrom dragged us all underwater.

Quintana runs all over the aquarium in hopes of finding more dead creatures to touch. I waddle after her, rapidly approaching my second child's due date. Another daughter. I can picture the scene in my womb during her future departure, when she'll abandon her ten-month vacation home via tsunami. I feel relatively confident in my ability to breastfeed her, to wake in the night with her, to care for her. We have baby clothes in a box in our storage room waiting to be laundered and folded. Yet I feel unprepared. It's birth that I can't seem to plan for, as though there were a true way to assemble one's body into a readied state to pass a human. So much depends on the baby's positioning and how she twists and contorts through the pelvis, the angle of her head as it propels through the birth canal.

There was a moment during Quintana's birth that clings to me as fervently as she did as a newborn. It was late afternoon, and my active labour had already surpassed a full night and morning. I hadn't felt the urge to push, but began as soon as my midwife gave me the okay, desperate to do anything to speed up the process. The ramming in my pelvis convinced me that death from childbirth might be getting off easy—I was sure my clitoris would explode, shards of eight thousand nerve endings rocketing off into the atmosphere. As my vagina stretched to accomodate Quintana's head, the globe of her was like an eye lifting and erupting from its socket.

In Greek mythology, there is a legendary monster named Scylla that lives on one side of a narrow channel of water, opposite her counterpart, Charybdis. There are many accounts of Scylla's descent into madness. In some versions, she sprouts multiple gruesome heads, each with snakelike necks and rows of jagged shark teeth. Sometimes her body consists of tentaclelike legs and a feline tail. In one telling, she captures six sailors off the deck of their ship and devours them alive.

With every push, the pain made me clamp my palms down against Quintana's head in a futile attempt to cram her back inside. As I pushed, it felt like I was sprouting my own mutinous appendages, the pain giving me a voice that could tear apart the birth team that hovered around me.

The final push lasted five full gratifying seconds. So pleasurable was the release of her head into the open air that I was in ecstasy. After her head emerged, her ethereal body paused, her shoulders obstructing entry into the world. Time froze as we both waited for that next contraction and I became mythical, polycephalic, a double-headed monster twinning with my unborn.

The French obstetrician and childbirth specialist Michel Odent argues that pain plays a crucial role in the physiological process of labour and childbirth. If you take away the pain with a medicated industrialized approach, you take away the process inherent in oxytocin, often referred to as the "love hormone," a powerful biochemical elixir that provides natural endorphins during labour and allows labour to progress.

"You cannot extract the pain and keep the rest. It's a chain of events," Odent says. "So the objective should be that women are in such an environment that they can make the birth as easy as possible."

I'm not sure where I stand on this. When I tried creating the environment to cushion the pain, the cosmos of it split open a torrent of fear. I hovered above myself, calculating how my body could withstand my daughter's release.

It couldn't, I decided.

I could only imagine the relief an epidural provided; along with the absence of pain, it seemed like a tether to the human world that I had abandoned. Pain is what I strived to escape from, what Hypnobabies promised me I could transcend, what I would have done anything to crawl out of, yet birth seemed to require pain as a guiding force.

Under optimal positioning and the best physiological and environmental circumstances, birth still requires a crossover into a murky and ambiguous state. Labour is otherworldly. *You're so beautiful, so strong, so safe.* I could hear the words Dennis whispered to me, but they were so far away, like he was speaking to me underwater. I was aware of his presence but couldn't access the comfort he offered.

I became unreachable, categorically alone.

Catalogue

When Quintana is two, she falls asleep quickly at nap time and I get to read. It is early July, and a heat wave pummels the city. Like most Vancouver residents, we don't have air conditioning. I am pregnant with my second child. I sit cross-legged on the floor in my underwear and a maternity tank top that barely covers my swollen belly.

The baby is currently head down, anterior, her spine lining the curve of my stomach, her sacrum wedged in my ribs. Every so often a hand ripples along my side as I read, a tickling internal massage. This might be the last time I experience those alien movements. I won't miss that feeling, my internal organs stretched to make room for fetal antics. Her skull is crammed deep in my pelvic cavity and I feel hiccups low inside my belly.

I read the first thirty pages of Sarah Manguso's memoir, *Ongoingness: The End of a Diary*. It is only ninety-seven pages and some contain only a few lines, like bites at a tapas bar, perfect for my waning attention span. The book spans Manguso's obsession with keeping a diary throughout her life and unpacks her fear of not recording every detail.

The baby has become quieter over the last couple of weeks, too big to undulate my belly with tumbles and rolls. Cells are still multiplying rapidly, but all her organs and systems are fully developed. She's simply fattening up now.

The word cell comes from the Latin *cella*, meaning small room. The smallest unit of life that can replicate independently. She is a small room inside me, occupying territory.

All the birth stories I've read end with the new mother's topographical exploration of her infant. They investigate every crevice, every fold, every smooth or wrinkly surface. I didn't know people looked with such wonderment at every inch of their babies. Maybe I was too tired to pay that much attention.

When Quintana was two weeks old, Dennis caught a whiff of something ripe and fragrant while he was holding her. He lifted her floppy arm and there was a yeast infection, raw and festering in her armpit. We had no clue how long it had been there. She developed acne at two months, her face and trunk coated with tiny white nodules, and I ignored it. She had cradle cap—scaly patches that are sometimes found on a baby's scalp—and for months I put off the recommended treatment of brushing her head with olive oil, as though preparing a steak for the grill, and combing out the flakes of crusty skin. The idea of slathering my baby's head with oil felt perverse, until I found out that cradle cap, if left long enough, can prevent hair growth. I sat with her in the bath a few weeks after her first birthday and backcombed her hair after the oil soaked into her scalp. The flakes came off with ease and her hair no longer stuck to her head with a greasy shine. Why had I waited so long?

I was lucky enough to know I wanted kids when I had them, to have that urge, whether it was born of biology or a desire for unconditional love or both. I wonder, now, how anyone who is unsure makes this leap. I imagine it only happens because we can't fathom how dramatically and irrevocably we will be transformed. Most mammals engage in the self-sacrificing behaviour required to care for their babies without so much as a thought. It remains in our evolutionary instincts.

I didn't pay close attention to Quintana's body because I was too afraid of what I might discover. My parenting approach was, for better or worse, to do nothing and hope everything was fine. This approach worked for almost everything except the cradle cap. And the yeast infection. That took apple cider vinegar applied twice daily, and a hair dryer to keep her armpit free of moisture.

After the first destabilizing months of early motherhood, so much of Quintana's data was stored in my memory that my brain became a second expanding womb—her first word, her first steps, the way her body stretched as she learned to walk and run, the sound of her voice, and now, the way she sings to herself in the bath, the colour of her hair when the light hits it.

My daughter loves the moon and points to it every time she sees it. When we cuddle on the couch, she spoons my pregnant belly's shape—I am the full moon she cradles when she is bleary-eyed and still waking from her nap. My body seems to fill her with greedy and delicious joy. When she joins Dennis and I in bed in the morning she takes so much delight and pleasure in tweaking my thick, meaty nipples. Sometimes she twists them like she's using a soundboard, adjusting the base, the volume. Sometimes she squints with intense focus, as though my nipples are barometers and she's determining the amount of pressure. Sometimes she grins and slurs, "I'm touching your nipples" like she's a drunk fourteen-year-old copping her first feel.

Given that my breasts will be out for public viewing in another six weeks, I'm not actively discouraging this behaviour. She finds my body fascinating. She counts moles and connects them like constellations, inventing a new zodiac. She traces the scars on my left arm, the ones left over from my brief period as a cutter when I was seventeen and depressed. She pushes her index finger against the pimples that surge on my chest and face in a hormonal rage. She fingers the bruise left behind from an old belly button piercing. Sometimes, when I'm fresh from the shower and before I can get a towel wrapped around my hips, she tries to grasp a fistful of pubic hair.

When she was a baby, I loved and loathed her constant physicality in equal measure. Now that it's been several months since she nursed, I miss those tiny eager hands. My daughter has learned to pat our shoulders gently, to give our shins kisses when one of us is about to go out. I put in my time to arrive at this stage of sweetness, of nuzzling, where she lends us her tenderness.

Unlike Sarah Manguso, I never kept a diary. Not seriously, anyway. I was given one when my family moved to Copenhagen for a year when I was eleven. I tried to keep a daily account of the museums we went to, the churches we saw, the architecture and culture, the school I attended. I only filled about a quarter of it before becoming bored. I tried again in high school, but my entries were sporadic, mostly angst-ridden accounts about boys and girls I had crushes on, people I thought I was in love with who hardly knew I existed.

I was, however, obsessed with photo-documenting everything. This began when I was around fourteen and continued into my late twenties. I used a film camera religiously, spending generous amounts on photo developing. I even worked at photography stores to offset the cost. When I was nineteen, a friend's mom noticed my passion for taking photos and let me borrow her old darkroom equipment—a black-and-white enlarger, filters, trays, and a timer. My mom bought me a film developer, chemicals for processing film and prints, paper, and a safety bulb. I blacked out the one tiny window in the laundry room in my parent's basement with construction paper, and spent hours in my new lab, agitating reels of film, hanging them to dry, and watching images form in the developer tray.

Photos of friends huddled around firepits drinking and smoking, domestic scenes of clutter, a hundred different close-ups of my face. I didn't fully understand the chemistry behind photography, so watching pictures come to life in a tray of liquid felt more like alchemy than science. I was bewitched.

I meet with Megan, my birth photographer. Over coffee, we discuss how I'm feeling about the upcoming birth. She is pregnant, too, with her third baby, due in September. The births of her two daughters were fast, her first only five hours from initial contraction to delivery. Her second took an hour and a half. Precipitous birth, they call it, when the expulsion of the fetus is less than three hours from the first contraction. She expects her third will be precipitous as well.

I tell her I've been feeling anxious as I get closer to the end of this pregnancy, and she asks what I'm afraid of. "Mostly the fear itself," I say. "Going back to that place of isolation. I'm not sure I can do it again." She smiles. She has a kind smile that warms her whole face. "You did so well last time," she says. "I'm surprised you're worried. You were so calm, so peaceful."

When I saw the photos of my daughter's birth, I was struck dumb by my own appearance of serenity. In some images I am smiling between contractions, blissfully resting my head on the side of the birth pool, like an image for an ad. Even at the height of contraction my face is violently beautiful, all raw energy and desire. I look like one of those women who claim to orgasm during birth. My memory doesn't match the photos or even resemble them. It wants to. It craves a cleansing of the actual experience. I felt that in order to birth a new life I had to risk my own entirely. In my body, birth paralleled death. I didn't think I would survive.

While I laboured, I didn't care about the baby moving through me, slow like butter melting at low heat. I didn't know a thing about her. I didn't know that she was even a her. I couldn't picture her during labour, and I didn't invite her to come out. I felt victimized by birth, like it was something happening to me, not something my body was doing and, according to every birthing book I read, was made to do. Even if I was made to do it, I didn't want to be.

I felt like a botched experiment. The expelled life on my chest felt more like wreckage. I didn't feel strong as I lay in my own blood and sweat, holding my newborn skin to skin. I felt depleted.

But the pain of birth did prepare me for the grief of my lost self. Pain deepened my empathy, starved my ego, and prepared me for the fear I continue to carry—the fear of not being able to keep my daughter safe in this world.

Pain also prepared me for overwhelming joy.

One night, during my last month of pregnancy, I dreamed I gave birth so easily I felt only pleasure. Manageable waves of tightening and releasing, a slow burn that rings the abdomen. Between contractions, I was light and full of air. I felt no sickness or exhaustion. When the pain was fierce, I grew three heads and eight arms sprouted from my torso. I held myself. There were no voices whispering around me. It was just me and my heads and arms, and everything I felt was clear and bright and full of love.

When it was time to push, the baby was born the same way I once saw a beluga whale emerge from her mother at the Vancouver Aquarium. Smooth and slippery—effortless. The beluga's head flowed perfectly out of her mother like an organ that is let loose, freed of the confines of the body. After her head was out, the rest of her body squirmed free. A trail of blood from the mother dissolved into the water as the calf shimmied to the surface to take its first breath.

Toward the end of Quintana's birth, every second contraction was less intense. It was during those less excruciating spasms that I moaned the loudest, that I felt the most sorry for myself.

There is a difference between pain and suffering.

I tell people I used a birthing tub, that I birthed my first baby at home in my own apartment, that Dennis put a note on our door apologizing to our neighbours for the noise. I say I ate Popsicles and took hot showers, that I squatted on all fours like an animal and screamed in the privacy of my walk-in closet.

All of this is true. None of this is true.

Hunger: Notes to
My Middle Daughter

The first week of your life stretches out like pulled taffy. It elongates with heat and time in a fog that floods the apartment.

Each night you sleep the most and I the least. It feels cruel. I set the alarm on my phone to go off every three hours. By the time I coax a few ounces of milk into you, I only have an hour before I have to wake us both to begin the cycle all over again. You sleep through everything: the heat and the clamminess of the air, my frustrated jerks in the night, your own hunger. The task of feeding you, of being the sole party responsible for your ability to thrive, is daunting. Where is your hunger? Mine has kicked in. I can polish off multiple pieces of peanut butter toast in the morning and then finish my toddler's half-eaten eggs and pieces of nectarine. I inhale the pastries my in-laws bring over when they come to visit. There are six lasagnas in our freezer, and every night I devour slices of thickly congealed noodles and cheese.

It takes me twenty minutes to wake you for each feed. I change your diaper, blow on your face, and tickle your tiny, curled feet. I drape cold cloths over your skinny limbs and pat your fleshy cheeks with the condensation from my water bottle. I get five minutes of sucking before you're unconscious again. I want to shake you awake. Instead, I go to the kitchen and pump for ten minutes on each side to relieve the throb from both breasts. When they are soft enough that I can lie down without pain, I curl up in the dark bedroom once again. You sleep deeply beside me. I stare at the ceiling. *You're not eating enough.*

You're not eating. Not. Eating.

This morning is rough. Everything takes eight times longer and is twelve times harder than usual. By 11:30 a.m. I'm falling asleep at the table. We've run out of coffee. Your dad promises he'll run out and grab some after he makes breakfast. He dices jalapenos for the omelettes. He grinds fresh black pepper and pinches coarse salt into the eggs. He slices mushrooms into thin moons. Each vegetable goes into its own tiny metal bowl, and he washes his hands between prepping each ingredient, meticulous in his hygiene. I watch him do all of this and my eyes sting from exhaustion. I want to murder his face.

I don't know what to do with the hours that you sleep when you shouldn't. Time is a body slipping beneath the surface of the ocean, forced under by the weight of each nursing and pumping session. Eventually, time stops thrashing and fighting and sinks like a stone. The bottom is murky. My chest aches. I flop back and forth, trying to find a comfortable position. I sweat excessively and fluid leaves my body at an alarming rate. I try to catalogue the days and nights, categorize events, but each day is a blur of light and dark, of feedings, of spit-up milk.

While I wait for you to wake up, my breasts become hard as rocks.

In the second week of your life, you rest your cheek against my breast, your tiny fish mouth slightly ajar. My nipple pokes out. Seconds ago, it slid out of your clamped lips and a trickle of milk slid down your chin. Your hand clutches the skin of my breast. My neck has a kink.

The sharp ping of my phone jolts me awake. My neck is on fire from the awkward position I fell asleep in. I clutch my phone and try to shift without waking you. My friend Jen has texted a photo of her six-week-old baby's head. I smile at his goofy-looking crown. Another text appears underneath the photo: *Does Ori's head look weird to you?* I don't really know how to respond. It does look kind of weird, but all babies go through weird stages. I text back: *I don't know, all babies' heads look weird to me.* I believe my own text, but then I stare at your perfectly formed head. You are passed out and I roll over. I keep forgetting I can lie on my stomach now. I also forget that coffee after

2:00 p.m. is a bad idea. My body melts into the bed, creating a large divot in the mattress.

Your dad thinks I'm a terrible co-sleeper. Every time he checks on you, he pulls the sheet off your face. I wake just enough to pull you into me to latch, the stiff mound of my breast softening with each gulp and swallow.

Another text comes in from Jen: *The nurse thinks he needs a specialist. She was a total bitch about it, but I think she might be right.*

When you fall asleep during the day, I try to access your birth photos, but the files are large and cumbersome, and they download at a snail's pace. Milk collects at the corners of your mouth as you occasionally suck on a phantom nipple in your sleep. You're more alert now and starting to actively enjoy nursing, which means I can ease off on the app I downloaded on my phone that tracks feeds, poops, and pees. This also means I can stop being so paranoid.

Your eyes scan from side to side while you're latched. They are a dark liquid blue, almost black, like octopus ink.

A photo appears, one of your head that has just been born, our midwife's hands reaching inside me to wrench your shoulders. My face isn't in the photo, just my body—a well-oiled machine.

During the third week of your life, all four of us go to see our new family doctor. Sure that you have gained weight, I'm eager to get you on the scale, but you've lost two ounces in the last five days.

Your sister begins to melt down in the doctor's office as the appointment drags on, even after she is given free rein over the box of stickers. Your dad carries her out to the car while I stay in the empty office and nurse. Letters of the alphabet hang on the wall in cheerful colours. I look down and your eyes are closed. In spite of my tears on your face, you have fallen asleep.

I read a memoir years ago written by a mom about her teenage daughter who had anorexia. The mom took it upon herself to do everything she could to get her daughter to gain weight. She made all her daughter's meals and snacks using the highest-fat ingredients she could—whole milk, butter, cream, and full-fat yogurt. She'd sit down with her daughter at every meal, watch each bite she put in her mouth, laboriously jotting down notes as to what her daughter ate and how much. Every day after school, the mom would make her daughter a homemade milkshake with vanilla ice cream, whole milk and coffee cream. At dinner, she'd limit the amount of vegetables to make sure her daughter didn't fill up on low-calorie foods.

For the next several weeks, we'll do our own version of this regime. I'll pump after each feed and give you bottles of hindmilk, the thick, fatty kind that comes toward the end of a feed. I'll hold you skin to skin to encourage nursing. I'll snack on oatmeal lactation cookies. I'll take fenugreek, an herb that boosts milk production and makes my skin smell like maple syrup. I will keep this up until I am half dead from exhaustion.

A year ago, your dad lent out our baby swing to a colleague, and by the fourth week of your life I need it back. For months I've been pestering him, but it was a low priority on the to-do list. Then today happened, when you and your sister took turns going in and out of hysterics. Something about motherhood or hormones, or just never having my body to myself, plunges me into a panic. Everything is both brighter and duller than it should be. My limbs jitter as though nitrogen is bubbling up in my arteries. I am both above my body, observing its descent into madness, and somewhere deep within it.

We walk to the playground as a family and your dad and I are silent. Somehow the swing feels like a legitimate thing to stop speaking over.

Later that day, you have a weigh-in at the doctor's office. Nine pounds and two ounces flash on the screen. You've gained six ounces in three days and a rush of self-righteousness floods through me. I skip to the car after the appointment, swinging you in your car seat like we are in a rousing chorus of *The Sound of Music*. I check my phone in the car and I have another text from Jen. *I was right about Ori's head*, she says. *My doctor is doing a neurosurgical consult with the team in Phoenix so we're going to drive down for an assessment.* My stomach heaves. How can a funny-shaped head result in a neurosurgical consult?

That morning your older sister fell on your head. It was my first time completely alone with both of you. I was changing your diaper on the floor of the bedroom while she jumped around on the bed, pulling the duvet over her head like a tent. I finished cleaning your bum and was rubbing ointment on a few dime-sized patches of diaper rash when the background noise became a commotion in front of me and a giant clump of rolled-up duvet slid off the bed and landed on your face. You began to scream and the duvet clump twisted and morphed into a monstrous creature that I heaved into the corner of the room. I snatched you up, praying I wasn't further damaging your spinal cord and contributing to any paralysis. Your sister unravelled herself, let out a piercing shriek, and ran out of the room. I tried to force-nurse you, watching and waiting for blood to pool and trickle from your eyes. I felt your head for cracks in your skull, imagining tiny lightning bolts in your cranium, fissures spreading to the fontanelles.

But you were fine. By the time your dad came home you were calm, still nursing, your eyes huge like they'd seen things. They seemed to say *Mom, did you know? The world isn't safe.*

Jen sends another text: *He's probably going to need skull surgery.* I start to reply, but then you stir in your car seat and I drive home instead, wondering how a surgeon can possibly slice into something so small, so newly formed.

In the fifth week of your life, every time I feed you, an aching river of milk flows from the opposite breast. I notice things I normally wouldn't. An insect the shape and size of my thumb rests on the ceiling. A sequined bead glitters on the couch. Small orbs of dried milk from your sister's sippy cup stain the laminate floor. There are new freckles on my arm, and a freakishly long hair growing out of the mole on my right wrist. While you breathe and gulp, a tiny bubble forms on the nipple on the other breast, then slides off and falls like a raindrop onto your thigh. Time moves sideways instead of forward.

Jen texts me a quick update on her son as I nurse. Ori has a condition called craniosynostosis. This is when one or more of an infant's cranial sutures (cracks in the skull) fuse prematurely. He will require endoscopic surgery, a procedure to open the affected suture to enable normal brain growth, and he'll wear a helmet twenty-three hours a day for three to six months. If the helmet doesn't mould his head properly, he will require open-skull surgery, a much lengthier process that requires an incision into the scalp and cranial bones to reshape the affected portion of the skull.

I am slow to reply to Jen and when I do my responses are banal lines like *oh god, I'm so sorry* and *that is so scary*. I can't figure out how to convey how stupidly helpless I feel. You are fussy and I channel my wasted desire into giving you a massage. I coat your skin with oil, and gently rub the rolls on your thighs and the thick trunk of your stomach. You become slick and slippery, like when you were first born and had a layer of creamy vernix caked on your back. You have a tiny birthmark the size of a grain of rice on your chest. It hurts to look at you. The image of a scalpel slicing into a baby's skull flickers in my mind like bad reception.

In the sixth week of your life, your weigh-in goes surprisingly well. Your hunger has been satiated. My hunger continues to throb in my stomach like an internal wound. I eat large spoonfuls of peanut butter right out of the jar, heaping bowls of cereal, sandwiches piled high with shaved ham and thick slices of cheese. Sometimes I'm convinced it's emotional. It's a bottomless hunger—I snack all day. I have no idea what I've eaten, but the fridge is picked clean, lacking the usual clutter of leftovers. Nothing stays inside long enough to go bad these days.

An insidious voice in my head tells me to watch myself, that I'll never lose this pregnancy weight if I'm eating everything in sight. Meanwhile, Jen wonders how she will survive handing over her new baby to an anesthesiologist, and then to a surgeon. How she will walk back to the waiting room and fill the hours while her three-month-old son is on an operating table. I'm disgusted with the lectures I give myself.

We fly to Saskatoon to visit my parents. I open their refrigerator every hour while I'm there, searching for something to sooth the trapped feeling I have from being in my childhood home. More peanut butter out of the jar. Blueberry yogurt. Oreos stashed out of reach from the toddler.

I eat mindlessly when I feel trapped, and right now I miss my freedom. Not only with time, but with my body. You are more attached now than when you were inside me. It's another world out here, another planet. Colic. Your screams reverberate in the chamber of my cochlea. Even after your dad straps you in the car seat and takes you on a drive, I hear phantom screaming. We give you probiotics and gripe water. We jiggle and jostle and carry you all day.

My body has never felt so fragmented, full of bad coffee, packaged cookies, and toast. I hold you in my lap after nursing, my nipples raw and shredded from your latching and unlatching. I now have oversupply from all the pumping, fenugreek, and lactation cookies. Every time you unlatch, I become a geyser, spraying everything within a two-foot radius.

At a picnic lunch by the river, I unclasp my nursing bra and instantly a powerful stream shoots from my nipple, covering the sandwiches and cucumbers and boiled eggs in a constellation of milk droplets.

During the seventh week of your life, the Toronto Blue Jays have a shot at making it to the World Series. Game 5 of the American League Division Series, Jays versus the Texas Rangers, has just started, and you inevitably begin to squirm, your lungs rested from nursing and ready for the evening's wail. I heave myself off the couch. No one pays much attention to us—this is our nightly ritual. I strap you into the carrier and begin my rounds, moving through the living room, past my family cradling beers and bowls of chips, their eyes fixed on the game. I march down the hall, hang a left to yank open the fridge door and grab a beer. I leave the fridge door open and continue through the kitchen with the intention of closing it on my next lap.

The game is full of suspense, and the living room is a cacophony of groans and cheers.

Ori's skull surgery is scheduled for tomorrow and I'm a bad friend. I can hardly manage my own care, let alone extend shoulders for friends to lean on. I hardly give him any thought hour to hour, day to day. I'm well versed in my own hell, which is not remotely unique or deserving of sympathy. It is self-inflicted. I *wanted* two children. I might even want a third.

Once you're asleep, I bounce in place with my laptop propped open on the kitchen counter, responding to an email from a friend who, weeks ago, sent me a congratulatory message on baby number two. Cheers from the living room keep us isolated, tucked away on our own island. Eventually, I unravel your sleeping body from the carrier and put you down gently in the baby swing. You are a small alien, a UFO, oscillating safely in my waking dreams.

As I sit on the couch to watch the last few minutes of the game, another close friend texts me. *I miss you*, she writes. *I feel the distance between us. It's palpable.*

Friendships grow necrotic in time. There are those with babies and those without. Those in crisis and those in limbo. Everyone is grieving for time spent or time allotted. I don't know what to say to my friend. I used to hate people who didn't know what to say, but now I turn my phone off and toss it aside, and watch the Blue Jays win six to three.

Erosion

"What do you think about dirt?"

I ask Dennis this question one night, after he has flopped down beside me in bed. His glasses are off within seconds of going horizontal and his face rests inches from mine, eyes closed. I've been reading an article on my phone on the current erosion of Easter Island. At my question he opens his eyes, which are the colour of soil rich with organic matter. His eyes and voice were the topographical beginnings of my attraction to him when we first met.

He blinks. "I don't know what you mean."

"What do you think about erosion?"

His eyebrows furrow. "Why are you asking me this?"

"Just…what comes to mind when you think about it?"

He considers this for a moment. "Beautiful rock faces…cliffs. And waterfalls."

"So, beauty as the result of erosion?"

He nods and closes his eyes again. I go back to reading.

Later, a line from the article burrows its way into my sleep.

Erosion is a natural process, but human activity can make it happen more quickly.

My mom's index finger has started shaking. I notice it while she sits on the couch watching *My Little Pony* with my daughters. It's subtle and I wait and watch to see if I've imagined it. I go into the kitchen to start the kettle for tea. When I return, her hands are folded on her lap, but after a moment, she shifts and her right hand settles on her thigh.

There it is, a flutter of movement, a small tremor. A split-second blur of joints and ligaments.

When I was twenty-two, I moved home for the summer between university degrees. My mom was washing dishes one afternoon, and a glass broke in the soapy water, slicing her thumb. I caught her in the kitchen preparing to bandage up the deep gash. "You need stitches," I said, but she waved me away.

"I'm just going to tape it up and it'll heal on its own."

Within three days her thumb was swollen and blue and she could no longer bend it. A week later, she had surgery to repair the tendon the glass had sliced through.

After I first spot it, I start to keep an eye out for the finger-shaking. Weeks away from her seventieth birthday, I keep thinking that she must have Parkinson's, or worse. When I question my mom about it, she sidesteps my concern, shrugging.

"I didn't really notice," she says.

Over the next few months, the shaking takes over Mom's whole hand, then both hands. I confront her during a family dinner one night, demanding she book a doctor's appointment immediately. She shrinks in her seat at my anger and mumbles how the shaking hadn't seemed that big a deal. "But maybe I'll try to book an appointment," she says, giving me a guilty half smile, hoping the moment will blow over.

In 2014, my mom arrives in Vancouver from San Francisco for a short weekend stopover to celebrate Quintana's first birthday, and immediately complains of stomach issues and exhaustion. "The presentation didn't go well," she confesses, having just been a speaker at an entomology conference. I press her on it, but it quickly becomes clear that the topic of work isn't up for discussion. "I just want to focus on my granddaughter," she says, dismissing me. Only she can't do that, either. She's distracted, unable to maintain basic conversations. She repeats the same stories over and over, or paces around the apartment, muttering to herself. I hear the names of work colleagues, references to grant funding, and hints of a problem she needs to fix as soon as she flies home.

"Something is seriously going on with your mom," Dennis says to me later as we lie in bed. This is undeniably true, but it feels impossible to approach this agitated figure, the woman who's been confident and secure my entire life, who now lumbers irritably from room to room.

My mom and her colleagues were once in a video that showcased her research on hairy canola. It was supported by a number of industry organizations, including Agriculture and Agri-Food Canada scientists at the Saskatoon Research and Development Centre. The video documents one of the most important research contributions of my mom's career: the development of a hairy type of canola that naturally deters flea beetles from feeding on seedlings. The video is called *Hairy Canola Meets the Crucifer Flea Beetle*. You can find it on YouTube. It's the only part of her research I've been able to understand.

I watch the video for the first time in years, marvelling at my mom's confidence, her eloquence as she describes what a flea beetle will do to a canola plant. I skim articles related to the flea beetle and end up at a site that explains the various processes that result in erosion. Abrasion, where sediments wear down rock. Attrition, where sediment particles collide and break into smaller rounded pebbles. Hydraulic action, the force of water that compresses air pockets into cracks in rocks that then expand and crack over time. Burrowing animals, such as beetles and worms, also contribute to erosion by displacing soil.

I'm crawling along in vain. I'm filtering through old landscapes, getting caught in the mulch. I'm sloughing my mom's displacement.

On the second night of my mom's 2014 visit, we play cribbage and she has trouble counting her cards. She keeps trying, but each attempt is feeble. She can't add up her hand and, when she tries to move the peg, she's noticeably confused. I'm confused too, unsure if this is just that tendency my mom has to tire quickly during games. Historically, the family tradition was to begin a game and watch her slowly fall asleep during the middle of it.

After multiple rounds, it becomes clear that she's unable to process how to play. Eventually, she stops being able to identify the cards or decipher what the numbers represent. She stares blankly at her hand. "You're exhausted," I say. "Why don't you just go to bed?" After she's asleep, I sit on the couch with a glass of wine and wait for Dennis to finish putting Quintana to bed. He comes into the living room and I look up at him.

"Something's really wrong," I say.

My mom's the second-oldest in the birth order of her siblings. She was the stable one in a family of six girls, mother hen to her sisters. She married my dad when she was twenty-two, after seven years of being best friends. She was a few courses away from a degree in biology when my brother was conceived, dropping out when she realized she couldn't memorize scientific data while pregnant. She went back to do her master's years later and then a PhD after my sister and I were born. She received full funding, on the condition that she would begin her career at Agriculture Canada after graduating.

In the spring of 1988, my brother, sister, and I stayed with our oma, my dad's mom, in our hometown of Kitchener while our parents flew to Saskatoon to house hunt. I was a clingy kid and wasn't keen on being left behind, especially by my mom, though I got over it when they phoned to tell us they'd bought a house with a pool in the backyard.

As landscapes go, the prairies were a bit of a shock. While my parents were familiar with the flatness, none of us anticipated the stark beauty of the canola and flax fields, the contrast of lemon yellow and lavender against the looming prairie sky. My mom fell in love with Saskatchewan, with its shock of colourful crops, the way you could watch storms approach during the day and the northern lights explode at night.

The morning after our failed game of crib, my mom wants to contact her colleague to discuss the work crisis. She paces my living room, stepping around Quintana, who watches her with curiosity. I ask her again, "What happened?" She says she can't talk about it, but she's in trouble. "What kind of trouble?" She shakes her head, and I finally put the phone in her hand, as she did for me a decade earlier when I was in the midst of one of my worst bouts of clinical depression and couldn't bring myself to call my psychiatrist.

I give Mom my bedroom for privacy during her call, but hover outside the door, trying to hear what she's saying. After a few minutes, she comes out of the room and sits down on the living room couch. "Mom." She's unresponsive, so I say it again louder, as though it's her hearing that's the issue, but she's already gone somewhere else. She's stone-faced and rigid. "What if she's having a stroke?" I say to Dennis. He nods and pulls out his phone.

St. Paul's Hospital is less than two blocks away, but we drive because Mom can't seem to walk properly. She leans heavily on me for support in the elevator. Within minutes of arriving at Emergency, she is on a gurney and they are taking her blood pressure, inserting an IV, launching a barrage of questions as they examine her. She is catatonic on the bed, unable to tell them her full name or her birthday, and they rush her off to get an MRI. When they wheel her back two hours later, she's dozing. She's admitted and moved into a private room. "We'll be running tests so we'll keep her overnight," the doctor says. "We want to rule out anything neurological."

But they don't just keep her overnight; they keep her for four nights. During the day, her delusions spill over like stormwater runoff, an incoherent stream of paranoia. My sister calls daily from her home in Mexico. My brother flies in from San Francisco and spends the hours by Mom's bedside when I'm at work. She has always loved my brother fiercely, in the way that some mothers seem to love their sons—protective and forgiving of all flaws. She has almost normal intellectually engaging conversations with him, about philosophy and science.

When I arrive at the hospital after work, my mother pulls out delusions like a magician performing hat tricks. Within twenty minutes of my visit, she's convinced the Ministry of Health is going to convict her for defrauding the provincial healthcare system. She's sure she will end up in jail. "I'm a Saskatchewan resident and they haven't found anything on the MRI or my CT scans or any of the other tests," she says. "Nothing's wrong with me and they're keeping me in this private room that costs thousands of taxpayer dollars. They're going to arrest me for fraud."

My brother is calm as Mom spirals. He smiles gently at her and takes her hand. I respond with rational comments—the hospital wouldn't keep her here if they didn't think it was necessary, she pays taxes, is a citizen of this country, and has the same rights and access to healthcare as anyone—but my words only seem to agitate her further. Eventually, she ignores me entirely, turning to face my brother, taking comfort in his gentle demeanour, and blocking my existence at the same time. I watch as their eyes lock and Mom's panic slowly abates.

There's another type of erosion, mechanical weathering, caused by pressure release or plant root growth physically breaking up rock. Another example of mechanical weathering is frost shattering, where water spills into the cracks and joints in rocks. When the water freezes, it expands and the cracks are opened a little wider. Over time, pieces of rock can split off a rock face and large boulders can break apart into smaller rocks and gravel.

This was the decline of my mom after her breakdown—an eruption of anxiety spilling into the parts of her that once held calm, the cracks embedded in her widening over time.

I type my mom's name into the Google search bar for the first time—how have I never thought to do this before? Instantly, her extensive research history with Agriculture Canada pops up. There are dozens of publications with titles containing scientific and biological terms I don't understand, like *proteomic analysis* and *abiotic stress*. There are a few phrases, like seed priming, that I could comprehend if I stretched my mind, but it hurts, like my brain is going through its own biochemical transformation.

The next several links are all obituaries for other women who share my mom's name. A ninety-four-year-old woman from Swift Current, Saskatchewan, who passed away in 2011. A forty-nine-year-old from Camden, New Jersey, who died just recently. I find myself sifting through layers of links, spiralling into a cacophony of death notices, when all I wanted to do is find my own mother, vibrant and alive.

I slam my laptop shut.

My mom doesn't end up in jail. Instead, she is discharged from St. Paul's and flies home to Saskatoon under doctor's orders that she must receive psychiatric care upon arrival. The psychiatrist spends one session assessing her and then starts her on antipsychotics and prescribes Ativan to ease her bouts of panic.

Two weeks later Quintana and I fly to Saskatoon to celebrate my granny's ninetieth birthday. My mom has been planning this party for her mother for months, with family flying in from all over the country, all five of my aunts and most of my cousins and their kids. My parents' house is overflowing with family when Quintana and I arrive, but I find Mom, who was always a gregarious host, hiding in her bedroom, popping Ativan and sleeping. She hardly acknowledges my existence when I sit down next to her and rub her back.

At the party, my dad looks terrified for the first time in my life. "How is she?" I ask him.

"Oh, she'll be fine," he says, but his eyes don't quite meet mine.

My mom was always ready to take risks. She was the instigator of their 1974 Europe trip, when they spent a year travelling through over a dozen countries and living in a Volkswagen van with my brother. Dad was always risk-averse and cautious, relying on my mom's ability to push him out of his comfort zone. Now she seems terrified to interact with her extended family, and my dad is left to fend for himself. Everyone is bustling in and out of the kitchen and the living room, chasing toddlers, setting up for the party, or pretending to be busy. My aunts make all of the food. The cousins gather in the living room and watch our children play together. No one is quite sure how to approach my mom, so they don't, and she stays in the bedroom until the cake is served and we sing to my granny. Mom makes a short, bewildered appearance for the song, and then slips quietly away again.

I escape outside to share a cigarette with my aunt Patty, the youngest of my mom's siblings, and the only one willing to acknowledge the fire as it's burning. "Your mom's not okay," she says to me, an arm around my shoulder, tipsy from wine so I have to stiffen to support her weight. To me, this is obvious, but no one else seems to want to engage with the fact that my mom, who's never had a dip in her mental health for as long as anyone has known her, cannot get out of bed.

After the breakdown, and a combined diagnosis of catatonia and psychosis, my mother's health begins to decline. It's slow at first, the erosion, then a landslide rushing over exposed soil, dragging bits of it away. The meds dull her personality, make her tired. As a new mom, I'm tired too, with little energy to help build back up what had already been washed away.

Each time I fly home to visit my parents, I notice new details of degeneration. Mom is slow to respond and sometimes can't muster a smile. She often looks far away. She has trouble following basic conversations, or tells a story with full enthusiasm, forgetting that she told us that very same story earlier that day, and the evening before. Eventually, she begins to doubt herself when she speaks, her confidence shaken. The medication diminishes her paranoia, but it also pulls her into a lethargic fog.

Throughout my childhood and early adulthood, I saw my mom the way she seemed to see herself—invincible, and almost omnipotent. For most of her adult life, she would rise at dawn and work hours before my siblings and I would wake. She was in the habit of taking fifteen-minute catnaps in the middle of the day, but never seemed to require much sleep. After her hospital stay, she begins sleeping in until 10:00 a.m., getting up just long enough to eat a piece of toast in a haze, and then returning to bed for another hour. She naps long into the afternoon, relieved to disappear under the blankets and slip into a dreamless sleep.

On one visit home, about six months after her breakdown, I interrogate my dad, asking what Mom's psychiatrist thinks of how zoned out she seems. I question the type of meds, wondering if the dose is too high. "She shouldn't sleep this much," I say, as if I have any authority on how psychiatric drugs work. My dad shrugs. He just seems content that she's no longer having delusions.

A few weeks later, he admits over the phone that her psychiatrist weaned her off the drugs altogether. I absorb my dad's rationalizations of the psychiatrist's decision, his insistence that my mom is stable enough to be off her meds, in stunned silence.

When I get off the phone, I think of every time I've gone off my antidepressants, either with or without a doctor's help. The times in my twenties when I thought I was doing well and could surely manage my mental health on my own. The times I forgot to take my pills for several days, which was really a kind of intentional forgetting that so many do in the early years of being on meds. An active denial of our own mental illness. Mind over matter and other bullshit.

Denial is a type of erosion, too. A swift and sweeping declaration.

Vegetation has a large impact on soil's stability. Trees and plants anchor the soil in place, just as people in our lives do for us. Professionals guide us, families observe and act or do nothing, or sometimes make decisions for us, ones we may not be able to make ourselves.

When forests are cut down and grasses are plowed for agriculture and development, the soil becomes vulnerable, easily washed or blown away. Human activity that alters the vegetation of an area is one of the biggest contributing factors to erosion.

Two years after the first, my mom has another breakdown. My dad sees the signs early enough—the spiralling, paranoia, and delusional thoughts—and takes her in to her psychiatrist. She avoids the hospital this time, and her doctor prescribes new meds with instructions that she should expect to stay on them for at least two years, probably longer.

Three years later, my parents sell their house in Saskatoon and move into my apartment building in downtown Vancouver. They begin helping out with my daughters. At first, being with her grandchildren sparks my mom with renewed energy. She takes them for walks to the store for SpongeBob Popsicles. She watches them at bath time, passing them toys and playing water games, letting them splash her until the three of them are soaked and cackling. She reads to them at bedtime, doing elaborate and silly voices for the characters in the books. But, over time, she gives them less and less direct care.

My parents start a regular routine of collecting the girls from school three afternoons a week, but, eventually, my mom stops doing pickups. Now she waits for my dad to bring them home and gives them Popsicles from their freezer. She turns on the TV almost instantly, watches *Ben & Holly's Little Kingdom* or *Pete the Cat* with them, rather than playing. Sometimes she isn't awake when my dad brings them over, napping straight through until I come home from work.

Shortly after my parents move to Vancouver, I start a contract at a school desperate for a home economics teacher. Although my goal is to teach English and creative writing, I need to get my teaching career started and Foods and Nutrition 11 is my way in.

Over spring break, Mom and I take a short road trip to Portland, and, on the way home, I work on lesson plans while she drives. I share my desire to create a fun and challenging final project for my Grade 11 students. "Why don't you make a Prinzregenten torte with them?" Mom suggests, her eyes carefully on the road. "I could come to your class and help."

I love the idea. At the height of her academic career, my mom made a fifteen-layer Bavarian chocolate cake, the Prinzregenten torte, for an entomology conference. It was the same exact cake she made for many of my cousins' weddings, for my siblings' weddings, and for mine. This was her signature dessert, one she had become known for among her professional and personal circles. The cake was an epic undertaking, usually broken up into a two-day commitment, as each thin layer of sponge cake had to be baked separately, then cooled and stacked, with chocolate buttercream spread between each layer. Dark chocolate icing covered the entire cake, and each one was personalized, decorated to a specific theme. For the conference, she made an elaborate flea beetle out of fondant as a cake topper.

As June approaches, I'm in the thick of planning the last few weeks of school. Mom begins calling and sending me emails, requesting that I get back to her immediately about one or another setback she's discovered about the looming cake project.

"Are you sure you have the right type of pans?" she asks in one phone conversation. "Maybe we need to go and buy the round pans. We need extras for all the layers."

I suggest the students use cookie sheets to bake each layer, and then cut the large sections into quarters and stack them on top of each other. "The cakes will be rectangular instead of round," I tell my mom. "But that's totally fine." Satisfied that I've reassured her, I get back to work.

One afternoon, a week after the conversation about pans, Mom asks me to stop by her apartment.

"It's important," she says over the phone. "Can you come by as soon as you're home from work?" She sounds strange, panicked and removed at the same time.

"What's going on?" I ask.

"I just need you to come, okay? As soon as possible."

I stop by my parents' apartment, sweating from the heat and my own anxiety, juggling school papers and my laptop. Mom answers the door. "I needed to show you something," she says, beckoning me to follow her.

In the living room, she hands me a plastic dollar store bag. I peak inside and find a dozen measuring tapes. I look at my mother.

"What are these for?" I ask.

Her face is grim and her mouth is taut, like a line of the earth's crust. "I've been wracking my brain, trying to figure out how the students will be able to cut the large cake layer from the cookie sheet into four equal pieces they can stack on top each other," she says.

"You mean you've been panicking." My dad chuckles from his usual spot at his computer, in the middle of a game of backgammon against some online robot. Mom doesn't seem to hear him.

"They need to be able to measure the cake. It only hit me last night, when I couldn't sleep. Each group needs a measuring tape to be able to properly divide up the large layer."

I stare at her. There's no one around for me to mouth *what the fuck* to, so I let the words exfoliate my brain instead.

"So…you bought these? For my students?"

She nods. She seems pleased with her plan, but also agitated, as though bracing herself for the next natural disaster her mind is about to weather.

"Couldn't we have just eyeballed it?"

When we introduce the legacy of the cake to my students, we flip through a short PowerPoint with photos of cakes my mother has made for family members throughout the years, including the one for the entomology conference. There's a photo of a cake cut open, and you can see the layers of cake and buttercream, like complimentary layers of sand and soil.

As each group of students measure ingredients for cake batter and buttercream, my mom fades further into the background of the class. I try drawing her out, encouraging her to walk around the room and check out each group's progress. I invite her to answer questions about batter consistency and taste, but with each question she stands frozen in place, eyes wide and pleading like a frightened animal. Eventually, she retreats altogether, observing the chaotic energy of the Foods class from my desk in the corner of the room.

She never comes back.

My mom always found beauty in earth, in getting her hands messy. In the intricacies of alfalfa and canola. In the insects that would devour those plants, that needed them for sustenance. Now, the oceanic force of her has receded. Her legacy seems buried and her erosion almost complete. It's impossible to hypothesize, but I can't help it: What if my mom hadn't had two mental breakdowns in her late sixties? What if a generational degradation is inevitable? I wonder how I will erode—all at once or slowly, over time, to the horror of my own daughters—the sediment of what I know myself to be, loosening and washing away.

It takes months before my mom ventures to the doctor to ask about the finger-shaking, which has now taken over her whole hand.

He believes it's related to the antipsychotic she's on, a side effect that's shown up late. She has no other symptoms of Parkinson's, he says, or anything else that worries him.

By now, the shaking has stopped being the focal point for me; it's no longer the only thing I see when I see my mom. It accompanies the stiffness in her limbs as she struggles to get off the couch, the slowing of facial reactions, the blankness. And the cane she now uses to get around, its four stubby legs jutting out from the bottom of the pole. Without the cane, her confidence dwindles and she shuffles unsteadily to her destination. When my mom walks, with or without her cane, I can't look away—her body is stiff. Her shaking hands are knotted claws.

I have vague memories of going to my mom's lab when I was a kid. She would put me to work washing glass beakers and flasks, wearing gloves up to my elbows. Or she'd give me my own set of plastic pipettes and round petri dishes with layers of clear gel for growing bacteria. Sometimes she'd have me cross-pollinate alfalfa plants, using a toothpick to mix the pollen of one flower with another. I'd tie small identification tags to each pollinated flower.

Sometimes, if she wasn't busy, my mom would pull out a microscope and we'd look at cells together. I loved clipping the rectangular glass plate in place, peering through the ocular lens at the chloroplasts of a thinly sliced leaf, or a sliver of onion-skin cells, their nuclei treading gently in epidermal membrane. More than once, after explaining what I was looking at, tears welled up in my mom's eyes as she acknowledged the essence of each cell and its intricate beauty.

"Biology is art," she'd say to me. "That's why I love it."

I want to look through those lenses again. I want to find my mom's essence and cradle it, in all its displacement.

Fractal

At the fractal exhibit at Science World there are glass boxes separating butterflies, fossils, and leaves. Five-year-old Quintana and I examine the complexity of the butterfly wings, noting the unique dimensions as the veins subdivide. The wing pattern is a complex lattice of processes, timing, and genetics, and each element blends together—pigmentation, pattern size and shape, position—after the caterpillar enters its pupal stage.

Quintana holds a magnifying glass up to her eye, but doesn't know to bend down. She's instantly enraged that the butterfly wing seems so far away. Her hair falls in blond wisps around her small, fuming face.

Mesmerized by the never-ending patterns, we twist knobs and dials on a display case. Branches grow from the trees and twigs grow from the branches. This keeps going until we reverse the knobs and dials and the growth disintegrates.

She comes home from kindergarten and points out fractals in the laminate flooring and her stripey socks. In the succulents on the windowsill. In her sister's tangled hair.

Daily, Quintana thrashes her limbs at me and I can't retract my own violence. My fists clench. My voice is sharp. I sit on my hands to keep from smacking her. She beats her wings and there's a 6.4 earthquake in California.

She says, "I'll laugh when you're dead. I'll cut you. I'll push you off the balcony. You'll be sad when I kill you."

Can a dead mother be sad?

Dennis, fresh from the shower, sits on the floor in his underwear and holds her while she thrashes against his large, damp body. It's 8:55 a.m. We're in a state of disorder. We're late for school again.

Chaos explores the transitions that exist between order and disorder, which often occur in surprising ways. Anger erupts from my daughter with ease. She spews it, volcanically, in every direction.

Dennis and I sit in the windowless office of our daughter's psychologist, Janine. Neither of us says it, but we both fear the session isn't worth the $200 we shelled out, that we'll leave with nothing to show for it. After answering dozens of questions about the interactions between us and our daughter, between our daughter and her friends, her sister, and her extended family, after revealing our lack of parenting strategies and complaining bitterly that our home life is just *fucking hard* and basically *poor us*, Janine agrees that we could use some help.

"Most of us live at about here," she says, raising a hand and holding it flat in front of her chest, "and it sounds like Quintana lives right about here," she raises her other hand several inches above the first, until it's hovering in the air at eye level. "Her anxiety level means she's experiencing things at a higher frequency. A flurry of activity and noises can overwhelm her."

Kindergarten begins in September. Kindergarten ends in June. Grade 1 begins in September. Transitions are fractals.

My mom has five sisters. When they're together, their personalities magnify, become larger than life. They cackle and sing and dance. They cry intricate tributaries of their mother. Each one has been incapacitated by panic. Each one has been swallowed by denial. I hear about these lapses through my mom's fragmented telling. Through the secret emails of cousins, their daughters. Through confessional Christmas letters from aunts.

I use my own therapy as an excuse to abandon my daughter. I schedule appointments during her peak rage times and make sure the clinic is an hour away by bike. I cycle to save the environment, I tell myself. Afterward, I stay late at the Lonsdale Quay, order maki rolls and dip them into wasabi paste—the fever in my mouth, a purification.

Some days Quintana launches herself naked at me. Her movements are quick and agile. Spastic. She's out for the kill.

Fractals are most commonly found in nature:

Trees, rivers, coastlines, mountains, *dumb mom*, clouds, seashells, fiddleheads, geckos' feet, lightning bolts, Romanesco broccoli, *you're just a dumb mom*, Queen Anne's lace, peacocks, snowflakes, pineapples, systems of blood vessels, *you're dumb and stupid*, crystals, sea urchins, stalagmites, stalactites, hurricanes, *you stupid dumb mom*. Daughters.

We tell Janine about Quintana's tics: the eye-blinking, the coughing between each word, the licking her lower lip until it scabs. How, when we speak at the same time, she covers her ears with her hands and screams, unable to absorb anything we say, though we've had her hearing checked twice and both times she tested perfectly. How we had to buy $75 Hunter rain boots because they have a special flexible rubber that allow her to curl her toes like snails.

"You bring that up a lot," Dennis says to me after the session.

"Well, it's a fuck-ton of money to spend on kids' rain boots," I say.

At night Quintana begs to sleep with me. In the king-size bed, she folds her limbs around mine and clings to me in the dark. Her tiny feet imprint crystals between my calves. We exist as information for a new study.

The brain is organized fractally. It branches inward, thousands of pyramidal neurons clustered in its forest, like a cosmic tree. Dendrites stretching and connecting. Synapses transmitting and receiving. Branch in, branch out. Loop back.

Just like that, a switch is flicked and she is perfect, or as close to perfect as we could order. Goofy. A lopsided bottom-toothless grin. She flops her head around with a brand new haircut, a bob requested after two years of a dedicated Rapunzel length. Her eyes are velvet, her touch soft, and I don't dare make any false moves.

We practise breathing at home and even that is a fractal. I search abstracts with titles like "Possible Fractal and/or Chaotic Breathing

Patterns in Resting Humans," questioning if patterns of breathing are consistent with the properties of fractal or chaotic systems. I come across the fractal model of human bronchi, play a YouTube video and watch the branching blood vessels and arteries feather out and pulse. I tell Quintana to fill her tummy with air until it looks like a balloon, and then to slowly let the air out of the balloon. It's a game we can do together. She breathes in and out, slowly at first, her rhythm matching mine, then faster and faster until her eyes dilate and she's panting and sweating. Then she hits me, a swift blow to my arm. She'd rather stay in chaos. Her anger and anxiety split from each other like two neighbouring water molecules that end up in different parts of the ocean. But even with great distance, fluids cannot be unmixed.

The veins in her arms subdivide and her wings are a formation of iridescent scales—her grandmother, her great-aunts, her mother, all nesting together, take flight. She dances around the glass display cases, flapping her arms.

MARTYRS

After I became a mom, stuff began to fall on me.

It took a few years for me to notice, a few more years before it became a regular occurrence, and even more time before it felt like a hazard. Eventually, I thought that perhaps I should be wearing a helmet or a hard hat around my apartment, or that I should outfit myself with a chest and backplate to allow for optimal protection.

I compiled a list of things that fell on me:

Tools. A measuring tape. A giant brick of Parmesan cheese that Dennis bought from Costco. A bottle of Shout. A jug of laundry detergent. Packages of instant noodles. The handle of the vacuum. My kids' puffy jackets, and other clothes shoved in the bedroom closet. Shoes. The circular blades of the food processor. Paper towel rolls. Bottles of bubbly water. Individual containers of applesauce. Picture frames. That tiny fucking *Ben & Holly's Little Kingdom* castle. Cans of tuna.

Puttering around my apartment became a contact sport. I needed to anticipate falling objects, slow down time in order to have the chance to react, to pull my body out of the way. I had to be on high alert at all times.

It was also my job to heal quickly and efficiently and quietly if I happened to get struck by something. To not make my daughters wait a single second longer for their Goldfish crackers, their cut-up apples, or their TV.

I Let Out My Breath

Week 20

I'm at the clinic for my ultrasound, waiting at the door in front of a huge sign that says STOP: PLEASE WAIT OUTSIDE FOR A NURSE TO ASSESS YOU. I answer questions about the precautions I've taken in the last several weeks and the potential risks of exposure, while the nurse with the mask and plastic shield over her face holds an electronic thermometer like a gun to my forehead. She allows me entry, and more masked health workers greet me. I take a seat until my name is called.

The tech brings me into the same ultrasound room I was in for my thirteen-week scan, the last time I heard the heartbeat. She instructs me to lie down, and the tissue paper crinkles and bunches underneath my lumbering body. I tell myself those kicks I felt might not have been anything more than fetal reflexes. The baby could be floating inside me with no heartbeat, and somehow that would have to be okay because there isn't the time or the resources or the ability to gather and grieve in a global pandemic.

After lying there while the tech prepares my naked belly with warm gel and begins moving the wand around, searching and searching, I ask for the only detail I really need. I try to turn it into a casual statement but it comes out stilted and stuttered, like I'm being strangled.

"The baby's alive, right?"

The tech nods casually, her eyes still on the screen, but she twists it so I can see the tiny baby flickering with movement. She begins pointing out parts of the body. I see the two oval moons of the baby's bum that morph in and out of focus like a two-dimensional hologram. There are wiggling femurs and a skull the size of my fist.

We've made it this far.

Week 19

"You're almost there!" A cyclist wheezes in my direction as she rides past in her spandex and click-in shoes, her tight, muscular body moving like a well-oiled machine. She thinks I'm a newbie to this seventy-degree road, with my leggings and ratty hoodie that's two sizes too big so it can fit around my belly. *I'm nineteen weeks pregnant, you cunt!* I scream after her in the movie of my mind.

The hill is long and steep and I'm not almost there. I clumsily dismount from my bike and start walking. Aside from my belly, which stretches widely under my shirts, I could almost forget I'm pregnant. I'm too focused on teaching remotely, on failing to home-school my daughters, on keeping my two-bedroom apartment from exploding with clutter. On weekends, I pass pandemic time by baking and cooking and slowly perfecting my new persona—homemaker on steroids.

I stop for a minute to catch my breath. My pounding heart drowns out the fluttering in my belly. Sometimes when the fetus is pissed, it gives me a real kick just to let me know it's still here, and, to my relief, still alive. Next time I stop, another six metres up, I consider bailing on this hill and finding a different route through the park, or at least sitting down and working my way through the box of cookies I have stashed in my pannier.

On my third stop, the woman speeds past me, going downhill now, and screams, "Go rainbows!" I give her the finger. Then I look down and remember that I am, in fact, wearing ridiculous novelty knee-high rainbow socks.

Week 18

A skin tag on my inner thigh grows thick and bulbous, like a slowly inflating balloon. Normally the size and shape and wrinkly texture of a flattened pea, its colour darkens over a few days and turns the shade of a punched eye. My razor used to glide seamlessly over the flap of skin, but the sudden growth and change in colour has me too nervous to shave. I cover it with one of my kids' Band-Aids, featuring Olaf and his goofy cartoon snowman grin, and try to ignore the painful pulse when my thighs rub together.

In my first pregnancy, a lump grew under my right armpit. I made an appointment with my doctor immediately, who deemed it simply a swollen and overactive lymph node brought on by hormone fluctuations. Now, when I switch to a fresh Band-Aid in the morning, I tell myself I'll call the clinic, but a simple trip to the doctor feels like too much to ask of a medical system that is petrified of an influx of patients.

There's no time for pregnancies in a worldwide crisis. There's no one available to test your protein levels or take your blood pressure. There's no one to check for fetal heartbeats.

Week 17

I come back from a bike ride in the rain and make hot chocolate. It's the cheap kind that you mix with boiling water so I can ration the milk for cereal and pancakes. This kind of hot chocolate reminds me of hiking the West Coast Trail. We'd boil water to bring our calorically dense packaged meals and beverages to life—seven days of Mountain House dinners, instant oatmeal, and coffee. A few weeks after we finished the hike, I tried a macaroni and cheese meal, relishing in the memory of those nights around the fire. Unsurprisingly, packaged camp dinners only taste good when you've hiked all day and you're practically delirious from caloric deficiency. In daily life, they taste like congealed cardboard.

I sip my hot chocolate. I didn't add enough mix. It's diluted in the way that time is.

The world is lonely and panicked right now, but there's something about growing a human that feels the extreme opposite of lonely. Overwhelmed, yes. Trapped, often. I know that *after* the baby is born is when the loneliness arrives. This is my third child. I know to expect the postpartum isolation, but what happens when the baby is due to arrive in the middle of a global pandemic?

I turn on the TV and put on the Netflix fireplace. I stretch out on the couch with a hand on my belly, hopeful for an early kick, while the virtual hand on the screen stokes the coals to make the fire spring to life.

Week 16

If I were to have a miscarriage now, it would result in a trip to the ER. It would likely involve a delivery of sorts, or surgery. It would be me, making decisions by myself, in a small room, alone.

Last fall, on a weekend trip to Victoria with my husband and daughters, I had an early miscarriage. I found out I was pregnant on a Wednesday and then, by Sunday at 5:00 a.m., I wasn't. I woke to cramping and blood, a future emptying out of me. I stumbled in a fog to a twenty-four-hour convenience store to buy pads and pain meds.

I couldn't go back to the hotel for fear of waking up the kids, so I hovered outside a coffee shop until it opened. When a father came in with his four-month-old daughter and snuggled her while drinking his coffee, I cried silently into mine. When I returned, everyone was awake and my daughters were begging for pancakes at the hotel restaurant and fighting over the remote control to the giant TV. I snuck into the shower to clean myself up, put on a fresh pad, and walked out of the bathroom with a smile.

My husband was devastated when I whispered the news while the kids zoned out watching cartoons. The next day he called in sick and spent the day on the couch watching endless episodes of *Top Gear* in gloomy silence. I couldn't get it together to make lesson plans for a substitute, so I took extra Advil and just went to work.

Mothers don't have time for miscarriages. We have to bundle our children in snowsuits and take them to the zoo. We pick up pads that catch fetal blood and embryonic cells while we're grabbing milk for the morning cereal. Our sick days are already used up from that time the youngest had a fever and wasn't allowed at daycare. We make birthday cakes and homemade chicken tenders and breast milk. We hardly get to use the bathroom alone. The kids barge in, questioning the blood in the toilet bowl.

Week 15

Starbucks is open only for "grab and go" orders, and everyone stands as far away from each other as possible. Sometimes we smile and nod. I use my hoodie sleeve to open doors. I make my four-year-old keep her hands on her scooter handles, or in her pockets.

Yellow caution tape wraps around all play structures and swing sets, so we head to Second Beach instead, taking a shortcut through Stanley Park. Even the giant alder logs that normally sprawl along the sand, usually crawling with kids, are stacked tightly and fenced off, piled on top of each other like the crabs in the tank at my favourite dim sum restaurant—upside down, sometimes sideways, a king crab always on top. They look sad, the logs. The crabs are too broken to be sad, no longer remembering life before the tank.

Signs are set up along the gravel walkway: ENJOY A WALK ON OUR BEACH, BUT STAY SIX FEET APART.

Week 14

To be pregnant right now is strange. Growing a human feels at odds with the physical distancing we've been required to do since mid-March, when schools clumsily transitioned to remote learning, restaurants and stores shut down, and everyone went into isolation.

I can't feel this fetus move yet—it's too early. The flutters deep in my stomach tonight are more likely the result of the nachos I ate for dinner, but at least I'm no longer on the verge of throwing up 24/7. My body is more or less its old self, albeit a slightly more rundown version, with something resembling a sack of flour plumping out of my middle.

My next midwife appointment isn't for two weeks and, even then, it's not urgent so it will likely be cancelled to reduce the risk of COVID exposure. Some parents buy their own Doppler to check the heartbeat at home, but I won't do that. I can't. I'd be checking every hour. I have to assume this baby's alive, just like I have to assume that isolating myself in this two-bedroom apartment with my family is doing the necessary work of our times.

Week 13

The ultrasound tech is new and sweet, with a blond ponytail and tortoiseshell cat-eye glasses. The computer is finicky and the monitor is not showing what it should. She brings in another tech to help. I try not to shift, but my bladder is at dangerous capacity.

This ultrasound is the nuchal translucency screen, meant to measure the fluid buildup at the back of the fetal neck, a marker for chromosomal abnormalities. I've never needed this type of screening before, but I'm almost forty now. My advanced gestational age increases all sorts of risks.

The fetus wiggles for the camera; it's so skeletally adorable my breath catches and I let out an unexpected giggle. The tech believes there's the typical amount of fluid.

The heartbeat is swift and comforting. I let out my breath and it fills the entire room.

The Smell of Screaming

Inhale

When Granny moved into my parents' house, my mom renovated the upstairs bedroom for her. She ripped up the carpet and put in laminate flooring. She painted the walls eggshell and had a new window installed. The old one that I used to sneak out of as a teenager was discarded. Granny's antique furniture was shipped from Kitchener, Ontario, where she had been living with my aunt for the last decade. When she arrived, it was fall and the weather was starting to turn. My mom bought Granny a thick, puffy jacket so she could stay warm in the backyard when she went out to smoke.

The sense of smell comes about through the stimulation of specialized cells in a body's nasal cavities—cells that are similar to the sensory cells of the antennae of invertebrates. The human olfactory system works when odorant molecules bind to specific sites on the olfactory receptors, which are used to detect the presence of smell.

During the years when Granny lived with my parents, routines were formed. She'd shuffle into the kitchen with her walker an hour before noon, demanding to know when her daily egg salad sandwich and fruit cup would be served. She'd remind my mom how she took her coffee—"One-third coffee, two-thirds cream"—as if my mom hadn't been preparing her coffee for the last thousand days.

Our sense of smell all comes together at the glomerulus, a structure that transmits signals to the olfactory bulb—a part of the brain directly above the nasal cavity and below the frontal lobe. The end result is a subjective experience.

Granny drove us all nuts with her demands and barking orders, her moodiness, her obsessive rituals. Her social interactions were a series of repetitive questions usually directed at my dad, who'd watch sports in the living room as she ate her meals. *Where is that game taking place? What type of sport is that? Who's winning?* Questions ran on a continuous loop for each person in her life.

When I came home to visit, I swear I could smell her worsening dementia.

While the human nose can detect over a trillion smells, there are about ten basic categories of odours that are systematically used for describing smells:

1. Fruity (all non-citrus fruits)

When I tell my workshopping group I want to write about bodies from the perspective of smell, there's an awkward silence. One writer finally says, "Yes, that's an avenue not many have explored."

I didn't get what she meant until later—no one really wants to contemplate how the human body smells. Especially with aging. With mental illness. In women's bodies. In pregnancy. In menstruation. In sex. In hormonal shifts. No one wants to think too hard about armpits. Genitalia. Feet. Or the odours that emerge when you're gestating a human. Or when you're in the thick of menopause and you're bleeding endlessly and soaking shirts with your own sweat.

Capitalism has its hooks in smell, associating a scent with a brand (or *scent branding*) to create a closer bond with consumers. Customers will recall the brand or product when they smell the scent. These scent logos, as they're sometimes called, embody unique brand characteristics. After all, consumers are happy to think of the baby powder smell of a slender neck or soft, freckled shoulder in summer.

Hair, if you wash it regularly, with a pear or green apple shampoo. The parts of you that can transform into man-made fragrance.

I didn't used to have a great sense of smell. It was handy when I had cats; the litter box never bothered me. If I walked past a particularly smelly bin of garbage, it wouldn't make my stomach heave. Over time, and three pregnancies, I've developed hyperosmia, a heightened sense of smell. My threshold for tolerating odour has decreased dramatically, and I seem to be smelling everything.

Apparently, a decline in one's sense of smell is an early marker of mild cognitive impairment. I remember the smell of Granny's bedroom in my parents' house—stale Arrowroot Biscuits, mothballs. Dead air. Fermented flesh.

2. Citrus (e.g., lemon, lime, orange)

I'm unaffected by desirable smells and completely repulsed by anything else. It feels like a window into the next stage of life, where bodies emit their slow decay. I'm triggered by these odours, angered by the injustice of having to smell them.

Researchers can use olfactory tests to predict one's likelihood of developing dementia. In one study, participants had to identify five odours, one at a time, by sniffing a device that resembled a felt-tip pen, much like the smelly markers my daughters love to inhale. Cherry, blueberry, lemon. Toasted marshmallow. Black liquorice. All those candy smells, that sticky sweetness.

The five odours in the study were peppermint, fish, orange, rose, and leather. Peppermint was considered the easiest to identify and leather the hardest. I can't imagine going back to colouring after smelling a fish-scented pen.

I've started inhaling citrus to remind myself of vibrancy, of a body that's alive.

3. Woody and resinous (e.g., pine or freshly cut grass)

After almost a decade of Granny living with my parents, she was moved into a care home where, within a year, she passed away in her sleep. After her death, my parents moved out to Vancouver to be close to my family. They brought Granny's old antique furniture with them—the smell of those years of taking care of her imprinted on the vintage fabric and stained wood.

I learned recently that the smell of freshly cut grass is actually the smell of a number of volatile organic compounds called green leaf volatiles (GLVs) that are released when the grass is damaged. Anything can cause widespread damage: infections, insects, grazing animals, unintentional rough handling, or mechanical forces—like a lawnmower.

Some of the compounds released stimulate the formation of new cells at the site of the wound so it closes faster. Others act as antibiotics to prevent infection in the plant. The rush of chemicals emitted into the air (what we breathe in deeply and satisfyingly, known as "green odour") creates healing possibilities.

That delightful smell of a freshly cut lawn is actually the grass trying to save itself from injury. It's a distress signal. A cry for help.

I think we must smell the most alive when we're in the most vibrant pain. It's when we're numbed or subdued or broken—but functional—that we stop leaving a scent trail.

4. Chemical (e. g., ammonia, bleach)

As her dementia deepened, Granny refused to allow caregivers to help her bathe. My mom scheduled a healthcare worker to come and give her a bath twice a week, and Granny called the agency and cancelled every appointment.

I take one to two showers a day, depending on the weather and how physically active I've been. When I'm pregnant, I shower as many as three times a day, my own seasoned aroma seeping through my underwear almost as quickly as I can dress myself after. Gestational hormonal shifts turn bodies into petri dishes.

At some point in Granny's early years of living with my parents, my mom discovered that Granny had been cleaning her vagina with hydrogen peroxide during the daily sponge baths she'd give herself at the bathroom sink. Whether it was compulsive hygiene or more of a purification ritual, the bleach began to eat away at the enamel over time. The slow corrosion resulted in my parents having to replace the sink before selling the house.

5. Fragrant (e.g., florals and perfumes)

I had a disastrous Brazilian wax during my first pregnancy. I wanted a break from the hair that matted in the damp tent of my underwear. I lay on the cot, with my legs splayed as the esthetician decorated me with hot wax, and immediately knew it was a mistake. I didn't know that pregnancy increased blood flow to the skin's surface, resulting in highly sensitive skin. What I *did* know was that the wax had to come off. She was quick, flicking her wrist away from the hair growth, but the pain was an immediate ringing in my ears, like the screaming of shredded grass.

"I don't feel so great," I muttered, which was code for "I'm either going to faint, vomit, or shit myself on this cot." I sat up and put my head between my knees, hoping the wax wouldn't stick to other parts of me. The esthetician left the room without a word and returned with a glass of ice water. The wax smelled like honey, with floral notes and butterscotch. I imagined a cluster of bees swarming my half-bald vulva, searching for nectar to take back to the hive.

6. Sweet (e.g., chocolate, vanilla, caramel)

Though I have never fully understood this, the smell of newborn heads seems to trigger bliss in people. So many suggest fresh, milky-sweet innocence. Can innocence have a smell? Probably, but I doubt it comes in the form of a head that's barrelled out of a vaginal canal, or through the layers of muscle and fat of a torso. When I inhale a newborn crown, all I smell is an unwashed, slightly sour odour. Spit-up resin. The waxy remnants of cradle cap. I smell the postpartum exhaustion.

As a teenager, whenever my mom hugged me, she would breathe me in and whisper, "You smell so good." I never quite understood what the smell of my skin did for her, though I would swoon a bit from feeling that I had been so intoxicating to someone else. It was only when I had my own daughters and started smelling them that I began to understand how mothers need to breathe in their children. It's like burrowing your face in fresh earth.

My children's stink makes me instantly drunk. Their teeth, when they haven't been brushed in days, which smell of fermented fruit and granola bars. Their sun-bleached hair from hours of rolling in the sand at the beach, dried salt tangled in their briny scalps. Their browned skin.

The smell of my children is different from the supposed sweet smell of newborn heads. It's not that I don't appreciate the scent; it's more that I don't smell what others seem to. My newborns always smelled like me, like the ocean that regenerates itself from both the dead and the living sea creatures that make up its body.

7. Minty and peppermint (e.g., eucalyptus and camphor)

Your sense of smell is likely more closely linked to memory than any of the other senses.

My daughters bring me mint and basil from our patio garden. They make "summer drinks," where they pour glasses of bubbly water and add frozen fruit and dozens of mint leaves. I can see their hair grow, almost daily, and I smell the cells in their small bodies multiplying at rapid rates, healing scrapes and bruises quickly and efficiently. They bathe twice a week at most, less so in the summer, and somehow their bodies always smell like flowers and freshly butchered grass. The smell of fresh screaming. Of shrieks of joy.

8. Toasted and nutty (e.g., popcorn, peanut butter, almonds)

I used to go home to Saskatoon for extended visits in the summer and answer my own loop of questions from Granny: *Where do you live again? What does your husband do? How long have you been married? How many kids do you want? Have I ever given you an afghan?*

I have several afghans that she gave me, most of which are stored in the space under the sectional in my living room and have a permanent musty smell. Others were given away to old roommates. My fourteen cousins, my two siblings, and I have all received multiple afghans over the years, for birthdays and weddings and sometimes just because. The afghans were strangely perfect for movie-watching. I would bundle myself up in two or three, then let my bare toes poke through the holes, a large bowl of heavily buttered popcorn in my lap.

9. Pungent (e.g., blue cheese, cigar smoke)

Decades before she lived with my parents, shortly after my granddad died of a heart attack in the bathtub, Granny moved in with her sister, my great-aunt Kay. After two years of Granny's demands and tantrums, Kay kicked her out and refused to have anything to do with her. Then Granny moved in with my aunt Jackie and lived in the suite over her garage for the next decade.

Granny smoked in the suite, and the smell reminded me of when I was a kid and would visit my grandparents' Victorian-looking apartment, where Granddad would sit in his underwear, smoking and reading the paper. I don't remember him interacting with me at all, but there are photos of me when I was about six, with a bowl haircut and brown corduroy overalls, climbing all over him and laughing. He is smiling in the photos. I'm grateful for the documentation. Without it, the only thing I remember is the thick smell of smoke.

I was eight when Granddad died. At his funeral, Granny seemed petrified of her own grief. She instructed her daughters and grandchildren that we were under no circumstances allowed to cry at the service. My mother and aunts told their mother that she was not allowed to dictate how they grieved for their father.

Days after the funeral, Granny found out that Granddad had numerous debts. Devastated by the loss and overwhelmed by the financial burden she was left with, she tried to throw out or burn memories of him and their life together. She sold the family cottage at Sand Lake and instructed my mom and aunts to take boxes of photo albums to the dump. My mom promised they would. Later, she and her sisters divided up the memorabilia from the two boxes my mom stashed in her car—photos and letters from their parents' love story—making sure Granny never knew.

I can smell burning boxes in my sleep. I can smell my mom's tears.

I can smell the musty interior of the family cottage, the fresh cold of the lake. Leeches sometimes attached to us when we swam, sucking down our warm, copper-smelling blood.

10. Decayed (e.g., rotting meat, sour milk)

A few months into my third pregnancy, Dennis makes a roast chicken. I leave the apartment for two hours because the smell of an oil-slicked, rosemary-stuffed dead bird makes me retch.

Hormones marinating inside of me pour out every night, and I wake dripping with sweat. Droplets of fluid slide down my chest and arms, down the back of my neck as though I'd just stepped out of the shower. I lay a towel down on the wet sheet and go back to sleep, then wake up an hour later, having soaked through the towel.

When the sheets dry, they smell like a salt bed after the tide has retreated. Bacteria multiply and break down into an acidic pool, 75 percent contained in the beaker of my body during the day, and then flooding the sheets each night.

A baby will be born soon. She'll attach herself to the outside of my body and suck the milk from my breasts, leaving me soured.

Exhale

It's summer, and I'm nine months pregnant. Smells come stronger— both the good and the bad. I detect the slow death of bodies, even as I am growing a new one. Perhaps *because* I am growing a new one. My own body smells of sacrifice.

Granny was ninety-one when she was finally placed in the care home. I saw her once before she died. Miraculously, she still knew who I was, though she couldn't remember who I belonged to.

I hugged her skeleton. She smelled of nothing. She smelled of a mind gone, content in its departure.

Everything outside was fragrant and bursting with life.

Blood Month

In deep fall we turn into ghosts
—Alex Leslie

1st

Dennis and I are in a canoe fishing in the middle of a small lake in Lillooet, B.C. He throws cast after cast and I slump in the stern with my legs propped up against the gunwales. We only have one fishing rod between us, so we pass it back and forth. It's a perfectly calm day, the only sound is the conversation between two men on a dock across the lake, their thick Eastern European accents echoing along the water. The surface is smoother than polished sea glass, interrupted only when a fish jumps. My shoulders relax and I sink into the bowl of the canoe. Snow geese fly above us, heading south. I'm the background for the jumping fish, for the men who wave to us from their camp chairs on the dock, for this translucent, opulent lake.

We're on a weekend trip, just the two of us, no kids. This is the first year I've purposefully taken myself away at the beginning of this month, the first time I've made myself aware of November before we are halfway through and it's too late.

Though the fish are flipping their scaled bellies beside our canoe, we don't catch anything. The line tangles after only twenty minutes of casting. The wind picks up and blows us back to shore.

2nd

I love Wikipedia because it is written and rewritten by everyone, like a series of essays that the world creates together. I turn to it for information, but mostly for comfort, like a good book.

Today, I read up on November.

In Catholic tradition, November is the Month of the Holy Souls in Purgatory. Its adjectival form, *Novemberish*, means "dreary."

According to Wikipedia, November is designated as Academic Writing Month, Annual Family Reunion Planning Month, Lung Cancer Awareness Month, Movember, National Novel Writing Month, Pulmonary Hypertension Awareness Month, Stomach Cancer Awareness Month, Transgender Awareness Month, Pancreatic Cancer Awareness Month, and National Gratitude Month.

Its original name in Old English was *Blotmonao*, meaning "blood month," the month of heavy animal sacrifice, when early Saxons would stock up on food for the winter.

It's also been known as the month I am unable to get out of bed.

3rd

During bedtime, my children pile on top of my body, tackling me as though I were a receiver who just caught the ball. Their elbows and knees pin me to the mattress. The bunk bed is a cave I spelunk in. I thrash while trying to escape and stir up silt until I can hardly see. My daughters like to keep me on edge. The oldest one has a blister bubbled on her lower lip from repetitive licking. She has the same November disease that I do.

4th

What catches me by surprise each year is that this month is only thirty days. It lasts so much longer. It soaks into the city's stomach, ulcers lining the gutters of our metropolis.

5th

Our last family photo was four weeks ago, in early October. It was T-shirt weather, the sun bedazzling the sailboats in their slips. We had ice cream cones at Fisherman's Wharf. It's one of the few pictures of the four of us where everyone is looking at the camera and smiling.

If you count the embryo, we were five.

6th

One evening, early on in the month, I get a burst of manic energy. I make a roast chicken with a crispy skin that everyone eats. Nobody hits anyone or screams that they hate me. I do five loads of laundry, vacuum, and clean the kitchen. Suddenly zapped, I collapse on the couch with my oldest. Her warm, thin body pushes up against mine. She colours while I try to lift myself out of this slumped, narcoleptic body. Even on good days, I move through water.

7th

We've come up with a name for our possible future third baby, which means "deity of the woods." I think about the last time we tried, imagine the egg we lost as a tiny ghost circling its way back into my ovary to be chosen again on the right day, with a viable number of chromosomes this time. The little nymph haunts the woods, and my uterus.

8th

When I am twenty-six, I start taking antidepressants. I should have started a decade earlier.

After that first year, I will "accidentally" go off my meds about every six months, just to see if I can handle it. I can't. I try to wean down before I first become pregnant. The world is thinner, blurrier. I can't function. I go back up to my full dose.

One time, years later, I fly home from a week-long book tour with my eighteen-month-old. As we settle into our seats, I come across my prescription bottle while digging through my bag for snacks. I realize, as the flight attendants are demonstrating how to put on the oxygen masks, that I've forgotten to take my meds for five days in a row. Travel always seems to result in one or two missed pills from staying in different places and leaving the pill bottle in different bags each time. The flight is five hours long and my daughter doesn't sleep a wink. She's loud and clingy and needs me to dote on her like she always does. Her neediness makes my eyes burn. Her neediness is a swift punch. I sob silently in my seat, while she reaches across the aisle to repeatedly poke the man reading the paper. He's pretending not to notice us. I beg her to be another type of toddler, just this once.

9th

Alternative titles for this essay:

"The Weather Hates Us"

"Everyone Is Always Sleepy"

"Sure, There Are Some Great Things about This Month, Such as Veteran's Day and Leonardo DiCaprio's Birthday, But…"

"That Ominous Feeling…"

"Holiday Chasm"

"Penultimate Month"

"I Don't Mean to Be a Debbie Downer"

"Misery Index"

"Daylight Savings Isn't Saving Any of Us"

"November Rain"

10th

It is 1998 and I am about to graduate from high school. I take over my parent's basement and cover the walls with posters of Courtney Love and the Tragically Hip, paint a large calendar on one wall. I make a writing corner consisting of a coffee table with a large collection of candle-wax-coated wine bottles. Every evening I burn obnoxious levels of incense and write poems in my journal. After graduation, my friends all move out of their parents' homes and rent cheap apartments together. I stay in my basement room and stop seeing my friends. I start university because the idea of getting a full-time job terrifies me, but the most I can handle is three classes, the minimum I can take and still access my RESP. By mid-November I stop going to class and stay in bed all day, getting up only to go to my occasional graveyard shift at Subway. I assemble subs for the bar rush and wear a name tag that says "Sandwich Artist." My dad comes downstairs one afternoon and confronts me as I lay in bed, fingering my unwashed hair. He tells me if I don't start attending classes, I'm going to have to drop out of school, get a job, and start paying rent.

My hair is a thing of clinical depression beauty. It's bright red, hennaed from a box bought at the health food store, and so long that I can sit on it. I find dreads while combing my fingers through its unwashed glory, as if it's the wind-whipped mane of a wild horse.

11th

When I first learn about Anishinaabe soldier Francis Pegahmagabow, it's Remembrance Day and I'm showing a documentary to my Grade 11 social studies class. I'm also accidentally high from a student's edible, a piece of fruit leather he offered that I was too naive to refuse. I'm sitting at the back of the class, pretending to be engrossed in the documentary, but really I'm panicking. A spray of bullets erupt on the screen as we learn about Pegahmagabow's life as the top sniper in the First World War. My students glance over at me as I sit at the back of the room. They must know. I try to look composed as they exchange smirks with each other.

The average life of most snipers in the field is four to six weeks. Pegahmagabow made 378 kills and went on to be the most highly decorated soldier in Canadian military history. While I watch his bravery, lava churns through my body. After class is dismissed, I sit in my chair, thinking *what would Francis Pegahmagabow do?* He would do what he had to.

I teach the rest of my classes, attend the Remembrance Day assembly, and drive home still high. I make dinner. I kiss my daughters.

12th

Dennis comes into the bedroom and tells me that maybe he is too old for another baby. Too old and too fat. He just wants to run off to Texada Island off the west coast where you can bow hunt all year round. He'll bring back a deer carcass for our deep freeze. "How are you going to go on book tours?" he asks, running hands through his hair so it stands wild. *How am I going to go on hunting trips?* He's a lawyer. He's never returned with an animal larger than a grouse.

13th

Can I really be the milk and the warmth of another life?

14th

I've had a low-grade headache all day. I'm exhausted. I'm also looking at million-dollar houses on Bowen Island. I can't believe I'm looking at million-dollar houses.

I've kept myself afloat so far. I make a plan to consider meditation. I use my bike to sit with my emotional discomfort, my disembodiment. My legs strain in orbit as I peddle up the hills in Stanley Park. Small tears in the tissues of my calf muscles pull me back into my body. As those tears heal, my muscles will grow stronger, but for now, the pain is searing.

15th

It's raining. Even when it's not raining the expectation of rain is a heavy gloom over the city. The girls are on the couch eating fried eggs and watching old cartoons. Every so often one of them says, "I am Wile E. Coyote, genius by trade," and they both cackle. There is a numbness inside me as I listen to them laugh.

At night I watch sad shows to make me feel sad. I cry over families who aren't real. I've always done this, since I was a little kid. My favourite is *Six Feet Under*, a show that focuses on the Fisher family and their family-run funeral home. A person dies at the beginning of each episode, sometimes in gruesome and horrific ways, sometimes in ways that make me laugh. Every main character exists on the fringes of depression.

I've never seen death up close.

16th

Wikipedia tells me that dark matter makes up approximately 85 percent of the matter in the universe and is not to be confused with antimatter, dark energy, dark fluid, or dark flow. I don't know the difference between any of those things, but I know the matter is called "dark" because it does not interact with light. But dark and light do coexist, much like November and me.

17th

Focus on the positive.

Basic hygiene attended to. Apartment not overrun with silverfish. Kids oblivious.

Mind over matter.

Mind is a squatter in dark matter.

This too shall pass.

The cyclical nature of my mental illness means it is always passing through.

18th

I have a friend who texts me every year in the middle of November. *Just checking in*, she'll say. I blink when I read her messages. I never see it coming.

19th

Before Zoloft, it would begin like clockwork at the end of every September. I grew up in Saskatoon and the seasonal change was swift. The air became frigid overnight. The nothingness, however, was a slow build. September was innocent enough and I'd settle into the routine of classes and part-time work. October would come and I'd look forward to my birthday and Halloween.

November 1, I'd be in hiding.

20th

It's 2006. I'm twenty-six and in a bad long-distance relationship. This relationship exists somewhere between emotionally abusive and "just poor timing." He is older than me, and wants the same things I think I want: commitment, fidelity, babies. His thinking is linear and mine is all over the place. I desire fantasy that translates into reality. He operates within the realm of a very specific reality, namely his own. There isn't room for alternative perspectives. There certainly isn't room for an unmedicated November—when I sink into the dark matter of myself, he doesn't understand.

He comes to visit me in September and we kiss for the first time in my car on the side of the road and I feel his hardness beneath me. Until that moment, I didn't believe anyone could desire and commit to me simultaneously.

I fly to his city. I can hardly wait to see his home, the one I'll be moving to in just a few months. His apartment is tidy and well-kept, but the walls are concrete. The floor is made up of large, cold tiles, with throw rugs placed strategically around the living room to project softness. I begin to panic at the future that looms in front of me. Maybe I don't want all of this.

Unaccustomed to the digressions that depression takes, or perhaps too accustomed to it, he distances himself from my spiral. When I fly back home, the plan to move fizzles, as I'm unable to leave my bed. After days of not showering or leaving the house, my mom dials my psychiatrist and holds the phone to my ear.

21st

What matter forms my universe?

22nd

When I start antidepressants, it is January 2007, a few days after one of the worst snowstorms in Saskatoon's history. The snow blows ghosts along the highway as I drive to work. Drifts are mountains in the ditches. I open the camera store where I work and watch as white winds swirl through downtown. We don't have a single customer all morning. Weather experts urge people to go home and stay safe. By 11:30 a.m., stores throughout downtown are closed, and the streets are packed with cars slowly moving toward one of the many bridges in the city. For the first time in my twenty years of living here, they close the schools. I manage to back my car out of its spot in the alley and inch my way onto the street. With less than a foot of visibility, my usual ten-minute drive home takes two hours; I can't even see the rear lights of the car in front of me. I stop at a friend's house and watch the storm from her living room. *We are so small*, I think. My failure to thrive is irrelevant.

23rd

Dark matter forms the skeleton of November.

24th

I visit the man I was supposed to move in with a month after that snowstorm. I've been on medication for a few weeks by this point and am starting to feel positive effects. The heaviness in my chest has lifted somewhat, and I move through air instead of water. When I arrive in his city, I want to talk, to apologize for being the wrench in our plans. He doesn't want to hear it. He refuses to talk about the future; in fact, he refuses to say much at all. Some nights we watch movies, others we read on opposite corners of the couch. Some nights we have sex. He works during the day, and I spend my days in his apartment, wondering how I can make him love me again. One afternoon, I call my mom and cry so hard I use up an entire box of Kleenex. I hide the evidence at the bottom of his kitchen garbage.

The day I'm supposed to fly home, before we leave for the airport, he puts his arms around me. A peace offering probably, but I hope it's a chance to start over. I curl into him and let myself pretend we fit together. When it's time to leave, I beg him to hold me just a little longer and, in spite of himself, he does. Meanwhile, another snowstorm is seething outside, a slick layer of ice coating the roads. Already a cautious driver, he drives slowly, methodically, and we arrive with just forty-five minutes until my flight is scheduled to depart.

"See?" he snaps, gesturing to the security line that's crammed with passengers scrambling to make their flights. "We're late because I let you talk me into cuddling. This is why we're not going to work out. I ignore my instincts when I'm with you."

I miss my flight. Our drive back to his apartment is muted. He refuses to speak to me for the rest of the evening, and leaves for work the next morning without a word. His resentment fills every square foot of space between us. I book a train ticket to a different city to stay with a friend, and we don't speak again.

25th

It's November 2019. I find myself jittery. I read memoirs, self-help-type books, but my attention span is poor. One book tells me that progress takes place in the dark, when you aren't trying. Another suggests that it takes a certain kind of arrogance to assume that everything is invisible before you choose to see it.

I have a conference with a parent about a student with ADHD. "I adore your son," I tell his mother. "He's brilliant and charming and makes me belly laugh every day." We discuss how the ADHD brain functions. She tells me how in elementary school she would cut up his math homework so each problem was on a single strip of paper. After he solved a problem, she would put a check mark on it, then hand him another strip.

I want to write one sentence, one phrase, one word and hand each one to my mother so she can put a big beautiful red check mark on that strip of paper. I want to tape those pieces of paper together to make a new book, the way my eldest daughter tapes her paper sculptures together. That tape is her dark matter. You can't see it, but it's there.

26th

Dennis plans a hike through Stanley Park while the kids are at my parents' apartment. "A walk," he corrects me, because the swelling in his knee, his osteoarthritis, can't handle a hike. We're trying to make time to talk, to decide on this third baby. But then he calls me into the bedroom instead. "You always taste so good when you're ovulating."

We made our second baby the day news of the Jian Ghomeshi scandal broke. We needed a distraction, so we watched *Game of Thrones* and slammed our bodies against each other. It was ritualistic, barbaric. The only way to make a baby under those circumstances.

I found out I was pregnant minutes before I was about to open a bottle of bourbon. Earlier that afternoon I got a speeding ticket. I made a tourtière. The crust was perfect, but the meat filling was bland. It was an otherwise benign day.

27th

November acts as a tourniquet: The flow of life is restricted for the greater good. Side effects are soft tissue and nerve damage.

28th

I'm riding my bike. I wear my daughter's gloves, mittens with paw prints on them, the stubby fingers stretched threadbare. They just keep my knuckles from freezing, as wind whips the tiny hairs on my bare arms. I ride over the Burrard Street Bridge, past Kits Beach and the swampy water of the community pool, closed for the season. Past families wandering in slow, restless herds, then onto the gravel path that lines the ocean along Spanish Banks. Water swells against the base of the North Shore Mountains.

I breathe in and oxygen moves through my bloodstream. I'm dizzy with endorphins. My legs orbit the way forward, a rotating ellipse.

29th

There are entire Novembers I can't remember, whole seasons that my memory tries, and fails, to recall. November is an inverse of itself. A palindrome.

30th

My friend named her son Winter. I wonder, but have never asked, how often she cringes when people complain about winter.

I have nothing against winter myself. It's the end of anticipation. There's no expectation of growth or productivity.

Winter's the season to give in. It's recovery.

A Route That Does Not Include Your Child

I slam the door and immediately hear the beep of the key fob from inside the car, having tossed the keys in the front seat while strapping my youngest into her car seat. I know before I confirm the knowing, before I start yanking desperately on the car handles, my neck prickling. My daughter's eyes are wide, assessing my reaction, determining how to react herself. She knows something is wrong and starts to struggle, only to feel the constraints of the straps of her car seat. She starts to scream as I turn and sprint from the car back to daycare.

I've locked my thirteen-month-old in the car.

The biometrics and thermodynamics of babies and cars mix together to create a lethal cocktail. Known as vehicular hyperthermia, heat builds quickly in a small space and babies bake like bread. The body produces or absorbs more heat than it can dissipate. Once the body reaches a certain temperature, cells become damaged and organs shut down. A child's thermoregulation is immature, and their body's internal temperature will rise three to five times faster than an adult's. An hour or two in a hot car can cause permanent damage—or even death—to a child.

"Two decades ago, this was relatively rare," Gene Weingarten writes in a 2009 *Washington Post* article. "But in the early 1990s, car-safety experts declared that passenger-side front airbags could kill children, and they recommended that child seats be moved to the back of the car; then, for even more safety for the very young, that the baby seats be pivoted to face the rear."

This unintentionally created a whole new safety phenomenon for babies—Forgotten Baby Syndrome. Parents could no longer glance in the rear-view mirror and see their child. Out of sight, out of mind.

Parents often describe the postpartum weeks and months as a fog. By the time our first daughter was born, Dennis and I had both been awake for thirty-six hours straight. Dennis went to work the next morning and briefly fell asleep standing up at a urinal. I was averaging about three or four hours of sleep a night for the first six weeks. By the time Quintana was three months old, we were shells of our former selves.

While we managed to help our baby thrive, and even went on to have another one two years later, we knew luck played a part. There are so many variables to keeping a child alive. Parents live with sleep-deprivation, chaos, and the anxiety of responsibility—the gutting realization that it is all on *us*. Their tiny lives rely completely on our ability to keep all the balls in the air at once.

When we hit our late twenties, the brain's aging process begins and neurons decrease. Receptors are slower to fire. New parenthood also impacts brain matter, jump-starting a process called "synaptic pruning," which is the brain's way of removing connections that are no longer needed. The basal ganglia, a group of structures found deep within the cerebral hemispheres, function on a subconscious level through repeated activities—your ability to remember how to ride a bicycle, for example. In the case of driving to work, your basal ganglia want you to get from Point A to Point B, to the degree that they can override other parts of your brain.

The basal ganglia allow you to operate on autopilot.

Memory loss runs in my family. My maternal grandmother had mid-stage dementia for much of her elderly life, though she wasn't officially diagnosed until she was in her late eighties. When she finally received brain scans, it was determined that one-third of her brain had atrophied, the remainder floating gently in fluid and dissolving slowly with each passing day. My own mother struggles to remember details of conversations or past events. She adapts and works around this by documenting important interactions. She's an expert note-taker.

Before having children, I was confident in my memory. I recalled conversations, important dates, and events with ease. I chalked up any instances of forgetfulness to environmental stresses, or a stretch of clinical depression. Pregnancy changed all that. The early stages weren't too bad, but toward the end of my first pregnancy, I was forgetting everything. Most of it was laughable, endearing. Dennis would tease me about the way I loaded the dishwasher, as though I were creating an art installation—a plate wedged at an angle, a pot on top of the plate.

I was willing to chalk my memory loss up to pregnancy hormones, but when it worsened postpartum, I worried. I lost my keys six times in the first few months of Quintana's life. I misplaced important papers. Worst of all, I was completely inarticulate. There were times I could hardly string three or more words together to form a complete sentence. Experts call this "Baby Brain," which sounds cute, but I began to feel more of a kinship with those who'd experienced a brain trauma, or those immersing themselves in a new language. My head would pound. My tongue twitched. I ached to speak about my experiences, my feelings of identity loss in this newly acquired motherhood role.

My essence drifted helplessly inside me as though my body was an aquarium, as though my own brain was liquefying just like my granny's did.

The scenarios are simple and heart wrenching and none of us are exempt. Of the ones I've read, two continue to haunt me:

1. A man drives past his son's daycare on his way to the office. He's on a work call and his wife usually drops off their child, but she had an early meeting. He parks the car at work and doesn't notice the baby, who's fallen asleep still strapped into the car seat. Within a couple of hours, the interior of the car doubles in temperature from the summer heat. The man's

car alarm goes off multiple times within that first hour, likely due to the baby's struggling. The man hears it from his office window, but because he believes his child is at daycare, he eventually disables the alarm, annoyed by how sensitive it is. After work, he notices a crowd gathering around his car and assumes there's been a break-in. He approaches the car, irate at the commotion. It is only when he arrives that he realizes his son is dead in the back seat.

2. A woman thinks she's dropped her son off already, but she's only taken her husband to work. The baby, who has a cold, is dozing silently in the back seat. The diaper bag isn't in the front seat like it usually is. It's a perfect storm of circumstances. She misses the first call from the daycare because she's in a meeting and the call goes to voice mail. The daycare calls again, inquiring where her child is. She's confused. "What do you mean? He's with you." By the time she gets to the car, it has become an efficient oven. Crayons strewn on the floor have melted from the heat. Her son's forehead is a broiled moon.

Forgotten Baby Syndrome, like many afflictions, does not discriminate on the basis of race, class, or gender. Any sleep-deprived, stressed-out parent who takes a slight detour from their usual routine is at risk.

"If few foresaw the tragic consequence of the lessened visibility of the child…well, who can blame them?" Weingarten concludes. "What kind of person forgets a baby?"

Quite a few, it turns out.

In 2019 alone there were fifty-three deaths in the U.S. due to pediatric vehicular heatstroke, and those numbers are higher than in previous years. There's little published data on incidents in Canada, though according to information provided from coroners' offices and government agencies collected by *Paediatrics & Child Health*, six cases of vehicular hyperthermia deaths were confirmed since 2013. The stories are painful to read. In the worst cases, babies pull out all of their hair. There are cardiac arrhythmias and skin slippage, when blisters form underneath the skin. Seizures and swelling of the brain. Organ failure. It is a grotesque way to die.

While it is horrifying to read about what happens to these babies, I can't help but fixate on the parent who lives in the psychological agony of what their own exhausted brain has unknowingly allowed them to do. I'm not immune to the possibility of forgetting my child in the car. How can my brain *not* trick me when I'm borderline delirious from sleep deprivation, burnout, and anxiety?

When Tamsin was two, she began waking between 4:30 and 5:00 a.m. During the day, she would scream to the point where I wondered if toddlers could give their parents post-traumatic stress disorder. This went on for months.

One afternoon, to avoid another Old Testament–level meltdown, I searched for something to distract her in the car while we ran errands. The back-seat floor was littered with the inevitable Goldfish crackers and random toys, but I felt around the wreckage for a bottle of Advil I knew was there. Tamsin loved shaking it and hearing the rattle of the pills inside. The twenty to thirty minutes of rage-screaming that was sure to follow if I didn't hand over the bottle, combined with the desperation for a coffee, convinced me there was no way she could open it.

Together we drove around the city, checking off items on my to-do list while I sipped an Americano and she shook the Advil bottle the entire morning, happy as could be. From then on, I let her hold that bottle during every car ride we took, and the sound of the pills clattering inside became a soothing, familiar interlude.

One afternoon, we arrived home from a play date and I opened the back door to discover my daughter covered in small orange pills that littered her lap like candy. She held one in each hand and looked at me quizzically. I rushed her upstairs and called poison control. The kind nurse who answered inquired gently for Tamsin's age and weight, asked how many pills were in the bottle and what the strength was. I lied my way through the call, telling her my daughter found the pills in the bathroom while I was in the shower, that she managed to unscrew the top *somehow*. I don't know how many pills she may have swallowed, I said. Probably none, but maybe up to three or four? It turned out my daughter weighed enough that her body could handle up to twelve extra-strength Advil without having to go into the hospital for a toxicity scan. The nurse reminded me of the importance of keeping all medicine locked away and completely out of reach of my children.

"If it had been Tylenol, this would have been a different story," she said. I nodded into the phone.

In this case it wasn't my memory failing. It was my exhaustion and brokenness that dictated my actions. Or maybe I'm just a shitty mom.

Tamsin is five now and still a screamer. Her screams hijack my brain and hold it hostage. There are evolutionary reasons for this. I once looked up pictures of the brain under duress; side-by-side black-and-white scans showed an unpleasant response compared with a neutral response. Even the photo of the distressed brain looked like a face in pain. Screaming isn't maladaptive, it's purposeful. A baby's screams may alert predators, but they're willing to risk it because they need, more than anything, for you to hold them. It's an emotional and physical survival tactic.

When my daughter screams, I want to claw out my eyeballs. My amygdala is triggered and my cortisol spikes, and in those moments, I feel fucked. I'm absolutely one of those parents who could forget their child in a car; I'm human, after all, with a brain vulnerable to my environment. I am also a parent who knowingly leaves her child in the car, only for a moment, just for some relief.

The fire truck shows up within minutes and the whole ordeal is over a few minutes after that. Four rescue workers pry open the driver side door with crowbars and brute strength. They work quickly and efficiently. The fifth rescue worker waves and smiles at Dagney, saying, "It's okay, we're gonna get you out in just a minute," but she keeps on screaming and doesn't stop until the door is open, the car is unlocked, and I pull her out of the car seat and into my arms, both of us a hot mess, but safe together.

"We all have young kids," one of the rescuers piped up. "We've all done it."

They forgive me easily. It wasn't a warm day and I didn't forget her. I was right there, playing the part of the distressed, sleep-deprived, overworked, white cis mother, a sympathetic character. They're kind because they think I deserve kindness. They can relate to all the moments that led up to me being careless with my car keys for a split second.

One of the men returns from the fire truck with a Dalmatian stuffy wearing a fire hat and Dagney is thrilled. This happy ending keeps me from being steeped in shame.

But the ending could have gone another way.

I imagine it like this: something is off about the day, there are holes in my routine, and my basal ganglia take me on a route that does not include my child. My brain fills in the gaps—the importance of the forgotten child doesn't matter. When I fail to execute the plan, that memory is not destroyed, it's just suppressed. I don't stop at daycare on the way, but my brain creates a false memory of dropping my child off. Throughout the day I see pictures of my child on my desk, on my phone, on my computer. Colleagues ask about her stage of development, if she's cruising or full-on walking. I show a video on my phone of how close she is to taking her first step. I am at work. I am productive. My child is where she belongs, safe and happy.

I am absolutely certain.

MARIONETTES

Mothering young children is about making inanimate objects come alive. Waving them. Rattling them. Wiggling them. Making them sing or sob, giggle or dance. Giving them names and voices. Supplying dialogue. A heart and a brain.

When Quintana was a toddler, she'd do everything within her power to get me to play with her. She'd beg, negotiate, and cross-examine me into submission until I'd find myself on the floor in the bedroom holding a small plastic toy or stuffy and giving it an entire personality.

According to American puppeteer and director Roman Paska "any object to which people attribute life and energy" can be a puppet.

On the bedroom floor, Quintana and I infused inanimate objects with make-believe cortisol. We instilled rule-abiding amygdalas. We narrated elaborate backstories. But I soon realized our "play" was not an interactive experience. I had strings in my back that my daughter yanked at her whim—I was the puppet of her imagination and she was the puppeteer. The theatre of us laid out on a stage of her making. The script entirely in her head.

Quintana would feed me lines. I was supposed to memorize the dialogue quickly and then recite it back. Inevitably I'd screw up due to my own lukewarm investment in the performance, my mind wandering away and into an endless to-do list—what groceries we needed, what section of the apartment was due to be cleaned, what errands had to happen that day, and when the next doctor or dentist or eye appointment was scheduled. I would flub a line or a scene, and Quintana would fly into a rage.

"MOM, the dog is going to SCHOOL, not the STORE!"

We never achieved Quintana's end goal, though I don't know if she had an ending in mind. The game was conversation, expression, and dialogue—we never seemed to move through the plot in a linear way that prompted a climax. We wouldn't even make it to the rising action.

Quintana saw through my lacklustre attempts. She could tell I hated playing with her. She could sense my boredom. She would put toys and stuffies in my limp hands and direct me, but I had no enthusiasm. I'd rather scour my oven or have my teeth cleaned. I'd rather hide in the bathroom, pretending to have bowel issues, texting desperate messages to friends who were new parents like me.

I felt the obligation to perform motherhood, not so much for my children, or even my friends and family, but for the social contract I unknowingly entered into when I became a parent. Social media didn't help, with its condescending memes written in self-righteous cursive—*the days are long, but the years are short, being a mother is the most important job in the world*—cheap shots unleashed at parents who just wanted to zone out for five minutes.

As my daughter deepened her love of stuffies, dolls, and all things make-believe, I joked to Dennis that perhaps I'd just tell Quintana that I had pupaphobia, a fear of puppets, and that's what prevented me from being able to play with her. "She'll make you play anyway," he said, and he was right. She wasn't the type of toddler to care about my fears, real or pretend.

The way she relied so heavily on her stuffies and *Paw Patrol* characters did make me nervous. She seemed content only when directing the play and controlling the responses of her inanimate playmates. How would she respond to the friends she'd have in the future, humans who couldn't be controlled? If the way she reacted to my inability to play her games was any indication, I imagined her future social life would be sparse and lonely.

One of Quintana's most prized stuffies was a small green bear with a red-and-white-striped scarf, aptly named Green Bear. He was so tiny that he fit perfectly in her closed fist, and she took him everywhere. My friend Taran made a beautiful purple tweed jacket for Quintana and included a pocket specifically for transporting him. Green Bear was a crucial fixture in our family until, eventually, as many kids' prized possessions do, he went missing.

At first, we assumed he'd ended up deep in the crevices of the couch, or wedged under her mattress, and, as we looked, we explained that he was "around here somewhere." Quintana seemed satisfied at first, but after weeks of being unable to find him, she funnelled her rising panic into her second-favourite stuffy, a small black-and-white dog she called Chocolate Drop, whom she would drag everywhere, giving him occasional baths in the sink when his fur got too grimy. After a few months, it seemed she'd forgotten all about Green Bear. But every so often I'd find her on the floor in her room, surround by a sea of stuffies. "I was looking for Green Bear," she'd say.

The word *pupa* is Latin for "doll," but it is also the life stage of some insects undergoing the transformation between immature and mature stages. After binging itself on food in a manner that can only be described as disordered eating, a pupa must consume itself in order to grow. Hanging from a twig, the pupa molts into a shiny chrysalis and digests itself into mush. The remains contain organized groups of cells called "imaginal discs," which survive the pupa's cannibalism. Even before hatching as a caterpillar, it grows imaginal discs for each adult body part it will need as a mature butterfly—discs for eyes, wings, legs, and so on.

A friend tells me that a monarch caterpillar looks like the photographic negative of an adult butterfly. I'm charmed by this statement, thinking of how we often start off as the inverse of what we will become. Though it may seem to be languishing in this protein-rich soup, the chrysalis is deep in transformation. Motherhood suspends itself in a similar metamorphic cocooning—the result is a gruesome confinement and a complicated metamorphosis. The result often means taking a good long look in the mirror at your least attractive qualities.

As Quintana puppeteered, I became increasingly anxious. I could see how much she loved the power she held over her stuffies, and over the adults in her life. She'd throw me into her imagination, multiplying me into many selves. As I continued along my mothering trajectory, I felt simultaneously alive and deadened. I became afraid for myself. And then, of myself. I could feel myself shrinking, fragmenting. Disappearing.

According to Paska, when a puppeteer dies, his puppets are buried with him. I suppose we all need emotional support stuffies as we head off into the next world.

When my sister and I were kids, we played house. Though I was two-and-a-half years younger, I was thoroughly intent on bossing her around through make-believe scenarios.

Though our family was considered progressive—our mother had a professional career and made more money than our father—we were still kids of the eighties and there always had to be a mom and a dad. I made my sister be the dad, and she hated it. Eventually, she refused to play house with me altogether. This turned out to be the perfect solution for a game that could exist only in my unencumbered imagination. I could fully exploit my own whimsical brain, soothing myself with whatever fanciful story I desired.

I liked to wear a thin, faded flowery dress with an empire waist, which I thought closely resembled Laura Ingalls Wilder's play dress in *Little House on the Prairie*. I'd place a selection of Cabbage Patch Kids in our old wooden wagon and make my way slowly and painstakingly around the deck in our backyard, looping in a wide circle under the hot sun, pretending the small wagon was actually a full-size covered buggy. The dolls were my children, and we were on a great journey across the prairies. If my parents were to glance out the window while I was in the middle of this play, they would see their nine-year-old daughter walking the perimeter of the backyard with a genuine focus and determination. In my mind we were travelling through endless drought, a constant baking sun, and winds that blew so hard the wagon was in danger of collapsing. Food was scarce but we continued our journey. Unless it rained soon, we would run out of water. In reality, I was thirty seconds away from a television and a grilled cheese sandwich.

Unlike me, Quintana needed the game to be shared with someone, to have a witness to her imagination in order for it to fuse into a reality she could wield. Rather than play with her myself, I produced a playmate for Quintana, another daughter, Tamsin, just two-and-a-half years younger. Close enough in age to become a viable part of the story, but young enough that Quintana maintained complete control of the game.

When he explores the attachment to inanimate objects in puppeteering, Paska reflects on a performance enacted by a coffee bean and a match: a simple love story. During the show, the two objects developed character traits. When the coffee bean was lost in a pile of other coffee beans, and the match made an attempt to find the bean, Paska recalls that "the audience knew one was special."

"When the bean was ground up, it was heart-wrenching," Paska states. "The audience was almost in tears."

When I read this, I could see the single bean—its body like the hard shell of a June bug, skin slightly wrinkled, a fissure splitting down the middle—and felt a connection, even to the idea of it. I started looking at my own coffee beans differently, even at 5:00 a.m. when the playmate I produced for Quintana woke me up with her animated screams.

Since puppets are not truly alive, they can be used to work out inner conflicts, as my daughter's toys and figures did. Sometimes objects are safer. The inanimate connections we make are not alive, but neither can they leave us through death or abandonment.

When Quintana lost Green Bear, we assumed he was somewhere in the apartment we lived in. By the time we realized he was truly gone, Quintana had outgrown him in some ways, but she still spoke of him like he was a long-lost friend whom she hoped to reunite with. Even when lost, his legacy was such that she knew he was out there somewhere, waiting to be found.

Quintana is now almost ten, but sometimes out of nowhere she will sigh and then, almost in tears, will whisper under her breath, "I miss Green Bear."

Chimera

"At the beginning and the end of a life span, it can be difficult to distinguish mothers from daughters."

— "Separation of mother and daughter cells," Peter U. Park, Mitch McVey, Leonard Guarente, *Methods in Enzymology*, Vol. 351, Science Direct

Fetal cells are known to cross the placenta and enter the mother's bloodstream. They're found harbouring in the mother's body postpartum, sometimes for decades after birth.

A mother's cells are also known to host themselves in their baby's blood and tissues. This process is called fetal microchimerism.

With each fetus my granny carried, millions of embryos flourished. Some became my cousins, mostly daughters of her daughters. Some became my siblings. One became me.

Mom sits across from me. Vacant. Unwashed. I can't tell when she became divorced from her body. She hasn't noticed her own odour in over a year. Sometimes it is the smell of incontinence. Sometimes it's the smell of an aging mind.

It used to be easy, Mom and I, together. Talking. Or this is how I remember it.

My daughters play on the floor next to us. They inhabit the role of queen and princess and say things like *yes, daaarling* and *pass me the nail polish, dear mother,* and *princesses hold their teacups with their pinky finger out, like this.*

Whiteness plays out in satire, right on my chipped laminate floor. The pomposity of the British matriarch bloats under my girls' skin. The irony of colonial superiority—they didn't wash themselves either, just masked their stench with perfumes, linens. They resisted bathing. Masking was considered good hygiene.

My granny's resistance to bathing was well-known.

When my own daughters fight bath time, I panic. I tell them they will get rashes, diseases. I tell them they will suffer if they don't clean their bodies. Really, I am gauging my own level of suffering. I feel suffocated by this legacy of dirt.

I sip tea and oscillate: a pendulum of resentment and sadness. Mom and I resume small talk. Safe, banal topics—the girls' school, my job, a relative's recent surgery. Even with the superficiality of our conversation, sometimes my mom stops speaking and stares down at her hands unsure of how to answer questions I've asked, or perhaps she is just confused.

When she looks up, she reminds me of a prey animal. Her eyes are frantic, like I'm going to catch her in the act of something.

Below us, my daughters paint their fingernails. They drink tea in fancy bone china cups.

Maybe our relationship was never comfortable. Maybe I'm remembering it all wrong.

The family joke was that all my granny had to do was hang her laundry out on the line next to my granddad's and she'd get pregnant.

She had six daughters who lived, and one son who didn't. He died two days after his birth, and she never spoke of him. In the birth order, he came after Mom, who told me this when I became an adult. I'm not sure if he had a name.

My granny's last two daughters were identical twins. They'd escape from the crib and smear shit from their diapers on the walls. I think that may have broken her. She was harsh in her mothering, and downright cold to her grandchildren, erecting walls to ensure there'd be no obligations.

A chimera is an animal that has two or more different populations of genetically distinct cells, containing two sets of DNA coded to make two separate organisms.

These cells burrow in organs like the pancreas and the heart, and skin. They can live there indefinitely.

It's right about now that I understand how my granny anticipated the burden of all these generations she didn't intend to create.

When my granny moved in with my parents, she developed obsessive compulsive disorder. My parents had to secure the fridge doors with a U-Lock so she wouldn't rummage through it at night, arranging and rearranging applesauce containers. They gave her a clicker to use, but she preferred switching lights on and off. Locking and unlocking doors.

She was demented by then, but no one knows when her symptoms started. She wouldn't admit to memory loss, repetitive questioning, lying about medications, or incontinence.

By her mid-eighties, a CT scan showed that one-third of her brain was liquid.

Studies of female mice show that fetal cells that end up in their hearts develop into cardiac tissue. "They're becoming beating heart cells," said Dr. J. Lee Nelson, an expert on microchimerism at the Fred Hutchinson Cancer Research Center in Seattle.

These cells are not passive. They know where they're going.

When my granny was in her twenties, she was convinced she had a bad heart because she had palpitations. They were likely panic attacks. Her heart was fine.

It would be easier if Mom and I were close, connected. But in truth, I don't know if we ever were. I think I mistook physical affection for a kind of mutual emotional understanding.

Mom was shocked when I told her how most of my friends are uncomfortable with and often feel defeated by Mother's Day. "No one I know has a straightforwardly uncomplicated relationship with their mother," I said.

The irony of her surprise was like a layer of my own tongue peeling off. Her own complex relationship with her mother was completely lost on her.

Our relationship was lost on her too; the closeness I thought we shared dissipated as I cared for my mental health and she chose to neglect hers.

Memory is often how we wish things were.

I'm terrified that I've inherited a matrilineal selective memory.

Given the cellular link we share, I'm afraid my daughters will one day look at me as subhuman. Inferior.

Sometimes I beg my husband to tell me my worst characteristics. "I just need you to lay it out for me, okay?" I'll say. "Just tell me what my flaws are so I know I'm not in denial."

When I was growing up, I leaned heavily on Mom through long periods of depression and crippling anxiety. All through high school and into my twenties, I couldn't even go on a sleepover without an anxiety attack. I couldn't be away from her. I worried I would die without her close to me.

Maybe this is what happens when you become too vulnerable with your own mother—too needy. When you stabilize, she becomes the physical representation of the hatred you had for yourself.

I avoid thinking about this by being pregnant for the third time. Pregnancy takes a lot of focus. Babies are all work.

The animal "chimera" is named after the mythological creature, *chimera*, a fire-breathing, gender-fluid monster.

A hybrid being, the chimera is composed of parts of multiple animals:

A lion's body. The head of a goat sprouting from between its shoulder blades. A serpent's head coiling at the end of its tail.

My girls are fighting now. Dresses litter our apartment floor like discarded bodies. This tea party is getting political.

I sit at the table with my mother. I gestate my daughters' younger sister, my mother's youngest granddaughter, who gestates her own tiny eggs. Almost ready to split from me.

Soon I will have three daughters with the DNA and molecular structures and all the millions of fully formed eggs they will have for their lifetime.

According to myth, the chimera was considered "near invincible," with the strength of a lion, the cunning of a goat, and the venom of a snake.

Her deadliest weapon was her ability to breathe fire. A mother in her spare time.

What will my daughters pity me for? My memory? An inability to understand the nuances of emotions? For aging stupidly? Flaccidly?

Is this the place daughters always get to with their mothers?

I read once that the yolk of the egg isn't the chick, but food for the chick. This makes perfect sense and is also puzzling as fuck.

I'll be too busy to think about any of this for the next three to five years, at least.

How She Runs

An ache radiates from my tailbone and becomes like white noise, humming and flickering in the background. When I change positions, bend over, or go from standing to sitting, my lower back twinges. Sometimes the pain is simply a feeling of tenderness, as though I'd just finished an intense workout. Sometimes it's deeper, sharper. Occasionally it disappears momentarily, usually when I shift position, and for minutes, and sometimes hours, after I go for a walk.

As I stretch out in bed next to my four-month-old, my joints pop like twigs snapping in half. My body creaks and crackles, as tendons stretch and bubbles of oxygen, nitrogen, and carbon dioxide burst and release. My ligaments have loosened and the relaxin hormone that, as the name suggests, relaxes the body's joints to prepare for childbirth continues to surge through me for months after the baby is born.

I'm not used to noticing a particular part of my body so acutely, of being so aware of the ligaments and joints that connect to my coccyx, the base of my spine. It remains a bright spot from a blunt trauma, the place where my third baby rammed her head in a vain attempt to expel herself from my body. When the pain disappears, I feel that too. Its shadow forms a shape around where the pain has carved into me—a throbbing chalk outline. The shadow holds space for the pain to return.

I got my driver's licence right when I turned sixteen. After years of borrowing my parents' minivan as often as I could, I bought my first car, a 1985 Honda Civic named Agatha by the previous owners, friends of my parents who traded the car for six months' worth of weekly babysitting their toddler triplets. By then it was 2002 and the car already had over 300,000 kilometres on it.

I've owned a few cars over the last two decades, mostly used and in varying conditions, but I've never really known much about how they work. I can pump gas, top up the oil, and I could probably change a flat if I needed to. I can drive stick, an important point of pride, and necessity for anyone growing up on the prairies. It didn't occur to me until recently that driving a car around every day for the last twenty-five years without knowing the intricacies of how cars function is pretty stupid.

Most people don't understand the mechanics of engines; they just drive from Point A to Point B, and sometimes take their cars into the shop for maintenance. Many don't know the mechanics of their own bodies, either. That the sacroiliac joints, or SI joints, connect the hip bones to the sacrum, the triangular bone between the lumbar spine and the tailbone. The primary function of the SI joints is to absorb shock between the upper body and the pelvis and legs. Sacroiliitis is the inflammation of one or both of the sacroiliac joints. There are four root causes for this: traumatic injury, arthritis, pregnancy, and, in rare cases, infection.

I only learned about the SI joints recently, at forty years old, shortly after my third pregnancy and birth. This is not the first time I've learned of something much later than I should have.

Eventually, I bought my dad's old Saturn and sold Agatha to a friend for the $300 I paid for her. Before I handed her off, we sat together in the front seats and I listed off her quirks. She had a choke you had to pull out in a certain way or she wouldn't start. You had to pump the gas, but in a particular rhythm or else you'd flood the engine. Sometimes the driver's side door would lock on its own and the key didn't work well, so you had to climb through the passenger side and over the gearshift. I told my friend not to start her up and leave her running and go back inside—a common practice in the winter in Saskatchewan—because I'd done that a few times and it was like she didn't want to be left alone.

She'd lock me out and I'd have to call CAA to come and jimmy the door open.

I loved her, not despite these quirks, but because of them.

I go to a pelvic floor physiotherapist for the first time. I've given birth three times, and each time I wondered how my body would possibly recover. The first two times it managed, magically, like a well-lubricated machine. This time, months after the birth, I'm still in pain and it's getting worse.

The physiotherapist's name is Joanne, and though we mostly chat about our kids while I lay face down on a cot and she massages my glutes, I find myself attracted to her. Maybe because her hands and body are strong and she cycles to work, or maybe because of her short, bleached haircut, with one side shaved close. Maybe because she's my only hope for a body that resembles the one I once had.

She rubs and rubs, her knuckles and fingers kneading my ass like its bread dough, and I remember I promised my kids pizza and a movie tonight. "I'll see how much I can do externally," Joanne says. "But you might want to consider an internal digital massage." I nod my smushed face against the pillow. I don't exactly know what she means, but I have an idea. The baby, now six months old, perks up. She has just started sitting up on her own, her small body perfectly flexible. She babbles to herself on a blanket next to the massage bed.

A few weeks later, after the pain has reached a breaking point and I am hardly sleeping, I book an appointment with Joanne for an internal digital massage, which means she will treat my injured tailbone by inserting a finger into my rectum and slowly massaging the muscle around the bone that has been tense and stretched for months. I'm not particularly squeamish about my body, but this level of intimacy with a near stranger is awkward, even for me.

The feeling is strange, like something that could be sexual, but is simply functional, mechanical. It is only meant to ease my discomfort, to allow my body to function optimally again. Joanne tells me she has seen great results from this technique, and I'm hopeful. We chat about our kids, about our daughters' anxiety levels, what school is like now that all the kids are wearing masks.

When she's done, she leaves the room and I get dressed, marvelling at my ability to move and bend without pain.

I remember driving Agatha to work one morning, running late, and I took a curve in the road a little too fast. She hit a thick patch of ice, obscured by the inch of snow that had fallen overnight, and her wheels spun out. As we started to slide, time squirmed, unsure whether to speed up or slow down, and my vision sharpened—I was keenly aware of parked cars on either side of us. The road skewed as we looped around and around, three full 360-degree spins, until we ended up on the other side of the street, facing the wrong way. It was early and the street was quiet. This probably saved my life. We sat there for a moment, catching our collective breath. Then I gently pushed down on the gas, made a U-turn, and headed to work.

I don't know how long Agatha lived for, but it seemed as though she would have kept going forever. I was so broke back then, and had little money for gas. Even those times when she locked me out with the keys in the ignition, her little engine groaning apologetically, I couldn't stay mad at her.

I loved the way she'd run on seemingly nothing, on fumes.

Vigil for the Vigilant

Between 6:00 a.m. and 8:00 a.m., Dennis is out cold, his CPAP machine suctioned to his face. The machine's hose—our older two daughters call it his "elephant trunk"—coils from the mask, transferring oxygen into his nose and mouth to prevent apneas, or the involuntary cessation of breathing. The CPAP acronym stands for Continuous Positive Airway Pressure. The purpose of the machine is to increase air pressure flow in the sleeper's throat so that the airway doesn't collapse during inhalation. It also reports how many times in the night the sleeper has stopped breathing. A good night is three to four. A bad night is anything more, because any instance of your body refusing to breathe has an assortment of scary implications—an increased risk of hypertension and stroke, a higher likelihood of heart attack.

Dennis was diagnosed with obstructive sleep apnea when our eldest daughter was just a year old. A lifelong insomniac, he could no longer catch up on sleep on the weekends now that we had a child, so he went to a sleep clinic for the first time in his life. The clinic that diagnosed him determined that, without the use of a CPAP, he was having fifty or more apneas a night. Fifty or more instances of his throat muscles relaxing and his airway narrowing or closing completely. One of the biggest appeals of the machine was its promise to alleviate snoring, which had been a point of contention in our relationship for years.

The CPAP machine was one of a long list of things Dennis tried in an attempt to cure his insomnia. Nothing seemed to help much.

Sleeping pills left him groggy during the day, and anxiety meds didn't make a difference. CBD oil made him more anxious—not the oil itself, but the idea of taking something related to marijuana; he didn't want his senses dulled. Edibles, he downright refused, the idea triggering a defensive flare-up due to drug- and alcohol-addicted family members.

Falling asleep has always been his problem, not staying asleep. Part of it is the desire to have alone time, which is nearly impossible to come by in our family of five. But there's something else that's always been there, the part of his brain that throbs and spirals with worry. Sometimes it's about work, family, or finances, or just the general anxiety of being the primary breadwinner for a family living in Vancouver, one of the most expensive cities in the country.

It's more than everyday stress that keeps him up. He's also listening. He has one ear cocked at all times, even when he knows the rest of us are sleeping deeply. Even though we're on the sixteenth floor of our building and our sweet neighbours leave little treats for our daughters outside our door. Even though he's at most ten feet away from us at any given moment.

On a good night, Dennis will be asleep by twelve thirty or one in the morning. A bad night means its three thirty or four. On weekends, after I've made coffee and breakfast, broken up about a hundred fights between our older girls, fed the cat, and nursed the baby, I will put a mug of tea by his bedside, turn the white noise fan off (another sleep aid), and leave the door open so the sound of our daughters playing happily will ease him into the morning.

After his first marriage dissolved, but before he met me, Dennis began collecting knives. An avid bushcrafter, he'd carried a pocketknife around with him since he was a kid, but as he began acquiring knives, his interest quickly grew into an obsession. He collected mainly from Spyderco, an American knife company based in Colorado that pioneered features like the pocket clip, now common in folding knives. The impeccably crafted quality of the handles and their functional yet beautiful blades drew him in, and he began purchasing knives mostly from their tactical collection, some with silver half-moon edges, some curved dramatically at the tip like a fish hook.

By the time we met and began dating, Dennis was frequenting Warriors and Wonders, a local Vancouver knife store that carries Spyderco knives, and was on a first-name basis with Jay, the owner. Dennis and Jay spent hours reviewing features of different knives, comparing fixed blades with folding blades, determining the pros and cons of each. When I moved into Dennis's bachelor apartment in Vancouver's West End, he had over one hundred knives in his collection. Whenever we'd get ready to go out to dinner or for a hike, he'd peruse through the cardboard box where he stored them, choosing his desired blade for the outing.

Carrying a knife had become a necessity for Dennis, like a wallet or house keys. He never left the apartment without one fastened to his belt or slid into his pocket. It became a running joke with our friends and among his work colleagues. He took the teasing in stride but suggested that we also start carrying knives for basic utility purposes.

"You guys make fun of me for having a knife on me at all times," he'd complain, "but every time you need to open *anything*, you're begging to use mine."

Over time, I became used to living in a house full of knives. Dennis was always watching YouTube videos of experts showing off their sharpening techniques. Eventually, he purchased a sharpener that created such a fine edge that he could use it as a razor to shave hair off his arm. I regularly cut myself on our kitchen knives because I'd grown up with dull blades that squished the skin of a tomato flat.

After Quintana was born, we moved into a two-bedroom apartment and Dennis bought two matching IKEA glass display cases. He filled one with Royal Albert fine bone china, all of which he'd inherited from his mom after she died when he was nineteen: a pristine white teapot with indigo flowers spiralling around its body, a gravy boat, an array of vintage teacups and saucers. The other display case he filled with his knives; Spyderco tactical, opened and displayed on diamond-shaped holders, silver blades glinting when the sun poured through the patio doors of our corner unit early in the morning. Fixed blades perched majestically with their handcrafted oak, maple, or walnut handles, the fine grain of the wood honey-hued and cinnamon flecked. One knife had a handle made entirely of whale bone.

Dennis spent much of his early childhood on his grandfather's ranch, just outside of the small mining town of Greenwood. Nestled among a handful of other small towns along the Crowsnest Highway in southern British Columbia, Greenwood was a Japanese internment camp in the 1940s, and now has a population of just over 650. The main strip boasts one coffee shop, a handful of heritage stores, a small museum, three motels, and a family restaurant famous for its air fryer fried chicken. When Dennis lived on his grandfather's ranch in the 1970s, he and his brother and cousin roamed freely around the land, carrying their shotguns, searching for squirrels or rabbits to shoot. When he was eight, his mom moved Dennis and his brother to Winnipeg after becoming the first Indigenous woman in Canada to get her master's in social work, where she went on to open the first Native and Child Family Services Centre, Ma Mawi Wi Chi Itata, an Ojibway phrase that translates into "we all work together to help one another."

Dennis didn't use a gun again until years later, when Quintana was six months old. He started taking his mother's old shotgun to the Squamish gun range to practice. Soon he acquired more guns, keeping them safely stored in a gun locker in the hallway closet, the ammunition locked in a case. Safety was always his number-one priority, with self-reliance being a close second.

Dennis started hunting every fall, driving twelve hours north, up near Prince George. He slept in a simple tipi tent with no floor, a stove pipe poking out of the top.

After a few years of hunting, Dennis started going to an indoor archery range, where he learned to use a compound bow. "You can bowhunt all year on some of the smaller islands," he said, planning trips to Texada, a gulf island off the coast of Vancouver Island, where a lack of predators meant that mule deer were culled every year.

He started taking Quintana, six at the time, to the archery range so they could shoot together. She'd hold her mahogany recurve proudly, her right arm stretched back, poised, the index finger of her hand grazing her cheek as she glowered, unblinking, at the bull's eye. She was a natural. She began playing Robin Hood, with four-year-old Tamsin as her Maid Marian. The two would march around the apartment, each clad in makeshift garb, and Quintana would clutch her bow proudly, the three arrows Dennis bought her alert and ready in the quiver fastened tightly to her homemade belt.

Between the knives and the guns and the bows, friends joked that Dennis was the one they'd seek out when the zombie apocalypse hit.

During the second week of the COVID-19 lockdown in Vancouver, we took our girls down to Stanley Park. "If things get bad enough, I'll just bring my 12-gauge shotgun down here and get us dinner," he remarked as we watched a gaggle of fat geese make their way casually across Pacific Street, halting traffic as they sauntered toward the water at English Bay.

When everyone began panic shopping, Dennis was more relaxed than I'd seen him in years. I mentioned this to him, and he shrugged. We already had all the emergency supplies we'd ever need. Three ten-litre jugs of water stored in a closet. A large rubber bin full of non-perishables—cans of tuna, bags of rice, protein bars, and instant Mountain House dinners. We had dozens of rolls of toilet paper that lasted us through the shortage, though Dennis rolled his eyes at that particular brand of madness. As pictures circulated on social media of people pushing carts piled with Costco-sized mountains of toilet paper, he just shook his head.

"You can wipe your ass with just about anything," he said.

When I was pregnant with Quintana, before strangers could tell whether she actually existed or if my protruding gut was just a food baby, Dennis spent hours reading infant car seat reviews. He pored over safety articles, research coming out of Scandinavia that suggested that children should rear face in their car seats for as long as possible. Dennis took those studies to heart and Quintana rear-faced into her car seat until she was three and a half and had to fold her legs into the shape of a pretzel in order to fit.

We co-slept with all three of our daughters in an assortment of configurations—sometimes one parent with one child, sometimes the two of us with a baby, the toddler on a mattress on the floor, sometimes one parent by themselves in one room while the other slept in the bottom bunk of the bunk bed, squished in with the youngest. After Dagney, our third, was born, the older two began sharing the top bunk and Dennis spent most nights sleeping below them. This arrangement allowed Dagney and I to share the king-size bed we'd bought to accommodate our growing family, so I could nurse her easily without waking anyone up. While the plan was meant to allow for better sleeps for the baby and me, Dennis was relieved to be sharing a room with the older two.

"I sleep better this way," he confessed one night when we were discussing sleep arrangements. "If anything happens, I'm right there to protect them."

"Protect them from what?"

"Anything." He shrugged. "What if we had an intruder? Or what if one of them fell out of the top bunk and broke a bone and neither of us heard?"

"But we're on the sixteenth floor," I argued. "It's not like anyone can sneak in. And their bedroom window has bars on it." Dennis had the bars installed himself when we moved in, making sure they were narrow enough to keep a toddler's body from squeezing through.

"Anything could happen," he mumbled, turning on an episode of *Forged in Fire*, a show where competitors forge a knife in their own style from a variety of metal objects. "And what if I wasn't there? I could never forgive myself."

According to *Merriam-Webster*, the word *vigil* means "the act of keeping awake at times when sleep is customary." It also means "a period of wakefulness." Dennis continues to stay up long after the rest of us are asleep. He watches old zombie movies, YouTube videos on knife-sharpening techniques, and British comedy panel shows. Each evening is a vigil for his vigilance.

In September 2018, as I was getting back into teaching and our older two were starting school, articles began to surface on social media connecting Indian Residential Schools and intergenerational trauma. Quintana was in kindergarten, Tamsin was starting full-time preschool, and Dagney was only an idea, a window left open a crack for Dennis and I to contemplate, though our lives were already overwhelmed. I was teaching high school full-time for the first time since having kids, and my Grade 11 social studies class was in the middle of a unit on residential schools and cultural genocide. I invited Dennis to come into the class to discuss his experiences working on Indian Residential School (IRS) claims as part of the long-running class action lawsuit. Being both Indigenous and a lawyer for the Department of Justice, he was in the complex position of having the Canadian government as his client.

As part of the claims process, Dennis would go into a room with the claimant, their lawyer, and a judge or mediator, and following the prescribed claims chart, question the claimant in order to find out where they fit on the IRS abuse scale. This scale was intended to categorize the abuse into varying degrees, and then match that abuse with a dollar amount for compensation.

Dennis didn't say too much about the statements he heard, only that they were often far more gruesome than most people know. Sexual and physical abuse. Torture and neglect. Student-on-student abuse—learned behaviour from the abuse inflicted by the priests and nuns at the schools. The aftermath of children as young as five being taken from their families and beaten for speaking their languages or practising their cultural traditions. Resulting in alcohol and drug addiction, depression, and suicidal ideation. Intimate partner violence and parental neglect. Abuse cycles continued in families and along generational lines.

Often at these hearings, survivors would reveal what they experienced in front of their partners for the first time. One turned to Dennis and said, "I never knew this. I never understood why he would cringe when I'd touch him."

The term *epigenetics*, a relatively new phenomenon that has received mixed reviews among scientific communities, was originally coined in 1942 by embryologist Conrad Waddington. The *epi* of epigenetics is a prefix from Greek, and translates into "upon," "near to," or "in addition." In other words, epigenetics means "in addition to genetics," and is the study of how behaviour and environment affect the way your genes function. Waddington speculated that "a disturbance at an early stage may gradually cause more and more far-reaching abnormalities in many different organs and tissues."

This seedling of a theory was difficult to test for decades, until it was examined through the lens of the brief but brutal Dutch famine that occurred toward the end of the Second World War. In 1944, Dutch railway workers went on strike in an attempt to prevent Nazi troops from advancing into the Netherlands. In retaliation, the Nazis blocked food supplies, resulting in what is now known as the "Dutch Hunger Winter," a famine so pervasive that 20,000 people died of starvation within nine months.

New York Times science columnist Carl Zimmer noted the connection between the Dutch famine and epigenetics, referencing a recent 2018 study from geneticists that found that some genes were muted in unborn children during the Dutch Hunger Winter, and never awakened. "Because it started and ended so abruptly, it has served as an unplanned experiment in human health," Zimmer wrote. "Pregnant women, it turns out, were uniquely vulnerable, and the children they gave birth to have been influenced by famine throughout their lives." Research conducted by epidemiologists in the decades that followed showed that those children who had been in utero during the famine experienced high rates of conditions like diabetes and schizophrenia, and a 10 percent increase in mortality.

Dennis did what he could to get survivors the best possible outcome for their claim. An expert at finessing the bureaucratic language of the compensation scale, he knew what questions to ask on record and how to make survivors feel safe in the room, but hearing these stories devastated him. He has family who went through the IRS system—an uncle, an aunt, and his grandmother—none of whom talked about their experiences. His own mother managed to avoid being sent away, though he doesn't know how.

Vigil is also defined as "an event or period of time when a person or group stays in a place and quietly waits, prays, etc., especially at night." A group gathered in a public place to mourn a friend or relative who has died from a tragic accident. Grieving fans of a celebrity, holding lit candles, leaving flowers and photos in a designated spot. Family members keeping vigil around someone who is actively dying. Dennis staying up later and later.

When I lie down next to four-year-old Tamsin in the dark of her bedroom, she always reaches for my face. She insists that I lie on my side, facing her, and she curls her plump hands around my cheeks. She rubs my face with hers, sometimes gently, sometimes rough with desperation. Her desire for that end-of-the-day connection is a force stronger than us both. She runs her toes along my bare legs, scratching my skin, and I make a mental note to clip her nails the next day, but always forget. Her feet are small shards of ice and she wiggles them between my thighs and I squeeze them into my soft flesh to warm them. She thrashes around, trying to get comfortable, but if I turn to face the window, she'll hiss "Mom, TURN OVER" in a raspy whisper that is closer to a scream. Then she'll nuzzle parts of her face against mine— her cheek and forehead, her chin. Sometimes she'll rub her nose against mine, pushing her whole face into my neck. Her skin is indescribably soft. Her breath has a slightly sour smell to it, and I breathe it in because it is distinctly her. I breathe every part of her into me.

I didn't really understand Dennis's need to stay vigilant until my kids started school and they were away from us. I was teaching Foods and Nutrition, showing my students how to activate yeast for bread baking and how to properly manoeuvre the claw technique when chopping onions. I imagined what it would be like when my girls became teenagers, how much of the world they would be navigating alone.

Teenage boys are not really *boys*, except in the sense that they have no real understanding of consequences. But they know what they're doing. Those high school boys whom I taught to curl their fingers into a claw in order to keep them from slicing off their fingertips; their minds are worlds older than my daughters' small bodies.

I go through periods of anxiety that I can't shake, knowing full well that we live in a world built on the violence inflicted on women and girls. I don't want my daughters to go to sleepovers. One night I discovered a small bruise the size of a quarter on Quintana's inner thigh, and both Dennis and I asked her half a dozen times if anyone had touched her in a way that made her uncomfortable. After saying no multiple times, she looked at us as though we might be individually and collectively a bit stupid.

I sometimes look at Dennis and wonder, *could he hurt our children like that? Could I?* We talk and he says what he always says, "If I thought I was even remotely capable of that, I would take my own life." A valiant answer. The right answer. The one you want to hear from your children's father. But I can't shake this dark matter inside of me, this need to take all precautions, even ones that seem silly and overblown. The anxiety settles into me like it's come home.

When Quintana was two, she began showing signs of volatility, common among toddlers. A simple pjs-and-bedtime transition could quickly transform her mood into a full-on tantrum. One night she was screaming and flailing around as Dennis was trying to get her ready for bed, and she whipped a Nalgene water bottle at his head. In reflex, his hand flew out and slapped her face. It wasn't hard, nor was she particularly upset after, the tears lasting only a few minutes, but Dennis's guilt and grief rendered him inaudible. He later told his therapist what happened, and she spoke about the impact a stressed limbic system has on a person, the way in which trauma memories are imprinted on the brain.

"With cortisol churning through your system," she remarked, "it's extremely difficult to control those fight impulses that surface when your body and mind believe you are under attack, even by your own toddler."

When Dennis is startled, he reacts swiftly. If I surprise him by tapping his shoulder from behind, he will swivel and lunge, then stop himself with his fists raised, his body tensed in a fighting position. It's unintentional, and often looks silly, an overreaction. Under the option of fight or flight, his body chooses fight, every time.

Even as I write this, I feel anxious revealing it. What will people think? My husband is a loving partner and father, who uses his arms to hold and comfort our daughters when they are upset or scared. He donates his body as an instrument of imaginary play. He'll contort himself into a jungle gym, then a slide, and then a horse for our girls to ride enthusiastically off into the sunset. Tamsin's favourite activity is to jump on Dennis's back, driving her knees into his spine, grinning when she hears the groan of her impact. He's been blindfolded and tied up with paracord during a game of ninjas, then abandoned when the girls have grown bored and turned on the TV. Once, the girls yanked off his socks and underwear and hid them in the freezer, their wild cackles reverberating around the apartment as they ran around like banshees. Another time, I found him lying face down on the bed with his arms tied behind his back, like the victim of a vicious attack. They are brutal in their play, and he absorbs it all.

The etymology of *vigil* is from the Middle English *vigile* and the Latin *vigilia*, both meaning "wakefulness" and "keep watch," under the guise of devotion. It is also akin to the Latin *vigēre*, which translates to "vigorous." Dennis's surveillance of our children is vigorous, but *vigil* also means "to thrive or flourish."

Can a person thrive when they are constantly on edge, preparing and bracing themselves for the worst?

In Benedict Carey's *New York Times* article "Can We Really Inherit Trauma?" the author remarks that there can be an epigenetic explanation. "The idea is that trauma can leave a chemical mark on a person's genes, which then is passed down to subsequent generations." While this has become a contentious debate among scientists, as the biology has not yet completely caught up with the theory, many geneticists feel strongly that science will eventually lead to this seemingly wild hypothesis.

It took a full two months before Quintana stopped crying at school drop-off. Sixty days of leaving her bawling by the door, her small body quivering as other kids bounded past her into the classroom.

"Don't you dare let her see you cry," said Janine, our well-intentioned child psychologist.

Janine's auburn hair was always pinned fastidiously in place, her clothes giving the impression that they'd never been tarnished by baby spit-up or preschooler snot. Her tone was kind and compassionate, but her words were gutting.

"You can cry all you want when you're back in your car, but you can't let her see you upset."

We were instead instructed to smile brightly, provide a quick hug and a wave, then turn around and walk out of the school. It was gruelling and felt like abandonment, but we didn't want to be *those parents*, the ones who coddle or accommodate their kids' every whim.

It was worse with Tamsin. The tears would begin the night before, at bedtime, and she'd whimper into my neck, "Mommy, I don't want to go to school tomorrow, and I don't want to die." She'd become obsessed with death in the last few weeks of summer, and now school and death were synonymous with separation. At drop-off, she'd sniffle and cling to me for a few seconds, then take a deep breath and grasp the hand of Alicia, her favourite preschool teacher. "Goodbye, Mommy," she'd whisper, tears streaming down her face, allowing herself to be led into the classroom like she was being led to her own funeral.

After my own tears would subside, I'd drive over the Lions Gate Bridge to the high school where I worked and wonder where anxiety comes from. Everyone else's kids seemed to march right into the classroom without a second thought, while both my daughters crept in with their heads down, eyes on the carpet, wiping their noses on their sleeves.

How do our daughters work through what is going on inside of them when we don't exactly know its origin? Do we need to know the source of their fear in order to infuse them with strength and resilience?

In recent news, a mass grave is discovered with the remains of 215 children, some as young as three, at the site of the former Kamloops

Indian Residential School. None of my Indigenous friends are surprised. I'm not exactly surprised, either, but I can't seem to wrap my head around all those dead babies. But maybe that's the point, that it's impossible to process such a heinous legacy.

"I went off the deep end a bit last night."

I look up from my laptop where I'd been editing an essay. Dennis is looking at me, but also through me, to some faraway place.

"I pulled out my handgun and spent the night cleaning it."

I close my laptop.

"I wanted to be ready in case anyone came to take the girls away."

I tuck my laptop into the side of the couch. "Come here."

He shakes his head. "I have a meeting in five minutes."

"That gives us four and a half minutes." He nods. I shove the collection of small toys off the couch to make space for him. He sits down and pulls up his shirt. I put my hands on his back, a familiar connection we've assumed together for years. I run my palms over his skin, then begin scraping my fingernails around in circular motions. I can feel him relax into the back scratch.

"I know it's irrational. Crazy, even—"

"It's not crazy." I loop my nails around and around until it looks like someone has skated figure eights on his shoulder blades.

Dennis is the lookout of our family. He watches over our daughters, staying up later and later until night blurs and bleeds into sunrise. I wake up with the kids, break up their morning fights, and fix their toast or cereal. I change the baby's diaper and give her half a bagel to chew and drool over. When the girls run in and out of the bedrooms, leaving doors open and flicking on lights, I look in on him. Even in his deepest sleep, Dennis doesn't look peaceful. His body cocoons under the duvet, a looming shadow, his feet the only part of him exposed. His face looks pained, and even in the depths of REM sleep, stress lines crease around his eyes and tighten his jaw. When he does wake, it can take him a full hour to surface, his body lumbered into a sitting position on the couch while the kids climb over him and he tries not to spill the tea I've given him. When he stands, he sways a bit from the accumulative fog of bad sleeps.

Before he's up, but when the kids are in and out of the bedrooms, I always turn the light back off because I am his lookout, his watcher. But I struggle with this morning routine, with his insomnia, the ways in which it penetrates our lives as parents, his mental and physical health, and our relationship. It wasn't much of an issue before we had kids, but for the last eight years a mixture of rage and sadness gives me emotional whiplash each morning. I can't bring myself to wake him—those few hours in the morning are when his mind and body are at least somewhat able to rest—but I resent being the default morning parent and he feels guilty about it. We never quite land on a resolution. I want him to cure his insomnia once and for all, to develop a healthy evening routine, to give up his screens and meditate. Dennis wants his late nights, his quiet isolation after the rest of us are in bed. He wants to block the anxious thoughts that spiral like strands of molecules through his mind. He wants to be able to drift off quickly and without effort, but that never happens.

Dennis has lived with a sense of militant vigilance for as long as I've known him. He says he's felt this way for as long as he can remember. I can't help but wonder if trauma has silenced the cells he needs to feel safe and activated ones that keep him feeling on guard, like prey, crouched and ready. At night he's not only awake but tensed like a clenched fist. What can I do but watch him from the corner, light a candle, and hope that we're more than the sum of our genetics.

You're Wrong About

The windows of our 900-square-foot apartment are closed for the first time all summer. The stale air lingers, sluggish and recycled from my two daughters as they alternate between playing and fighting. We've been trapped inside for more than a week now.

Outside, smoke is everywhere. It looms against the glass of our sliding balcony doors like a shroud, barricading us in our own home. I am forty-one weeks pregnant. Every day, my belly contorts from the acrobatics of my third baby, and every night Braxton Hicks contractions harden my pelvis into cement. I leave the house for acupuncture and hook the toggles of a mask over my ears. Not only am I at the end of a pregnancy during some of the worst forest fires in West Coast history, there's also a global pandemic. I am trapped in my body. I am trapped in my apartment. I am trapped in the world.

At the acupuncturist's, I sob. "I can't do this," I tell her. "I can't be pregnant in the middle of a pandemic, and also be stuck inside because of smoke. One of these things has to end." The acupuncturist takes charge. She gives me visualizations to do, mantras to whisper. She taps needles into various points on my calves and ankles, one into my head and two into the soft cartilage of my ear, and then she leaves me alone on the massage bed, pins silvering out of me while I try to rest and visualize and breathe. After the session, she tells me to go to the woods.

"I know it's smoky, but go to Stanley Park," she says. "Sit among the trees and talk to your baby."

I drive into the park, leave my car in an empty lot, and walk to one of the many giant conifers that make Stanley Park famous, one that boasts a thick and sprawling root system. I sit and inhale acrid air deep into my lungs. The baby, my third daughter, is kicking hard, mostly against my bladder. To my right, about thirty feet away, three women in their mid-fifties have spread out a picnic blanket. One of them turns on some music and begins to instruct the others to dance with her. It's one of those hippy dance classes, about as West Coast as "avo toast" or the kombucha that's served on tap at the Second Beach concession stand. The instructor calls out to the women to just "dance their feelings," which translates into a lot of arm flapping and hair swishing and hopping around like Muppets. They sing off-key to the music, both tone deaf and unaware of the actual lyrics to the pop song that's blaring. "I'm sorry you have to witness this," I whisper to my almost-baby, as she kicks and kicks.

Contractions flare every ten minutes or so. They aren't especially painful yet—more like a warning, drifting through my pelvis like a slow blaze. I tell my baby that I want her to come, that I need her to come, but also that it's up to her when and how she does. I know this because her older sisters didn't come when I hoped, and the only way to move forward is to let all those expectations go. I say all this and try to believe it.

I sit there quietly, breathing through each contraction with my eyes closed, smoke circulating through my blood vessels. Then I stagger, wheeze myself up, and walk back to the car.

It's time to go home and have this baby.

In April 2019, my third book of poetry, *Q & A*, about the pregnancy and birth of my first daughter, Quintana, was published. A few months later it was reviewed by a woman who seemed perplexed—almost resentful—at my choice to write an entire book on this topic. Though she grudgingly admits my poetic memoir "arrives in the midst of a dawning realization that mothering requires a place in the arts and in life," she spends much of the review chastising the content of the poems, pointing out the many ways in which writing about pregnancy and childbirth should be reduced to only a poem or two, at most.

Of course, *Q & A* isn't only a book about my daughter's birth. It's about the ways women were historically treated in pregnancy and during birth, and how this treatment has informed motherhood. The book examines ways in which women's bodies were experimented on and used to advance medical science and reveals the birthing "tools" that were developed to extract babies in an assortment of horrific ways. It explores the barbaric phenomenon known as "twilight sleep," an amnesiac condition induced by an injection of morphine and scopolamine, developed in Germany in the early 1900s, and used to relieve the pain of childbirth. The suffering that many women experienced during pregnancy and birth as a result of this practice, as well as infant and maternal injury and mortality risks, is one of the prominent themes in the book.

Still, the reviewer is unimpressed. Not with the writing itself, but with my in-depth focus on the subject. She questions how I could manage to write a whole book on a topic that she feels would exclude men or anyone who hasn't birthed a baby. She wonders who would want to read a book that forces the reader down an *Alice in Wonderland*–style hole of bodily functions, extreme pain, fear, and a host of gruesome physiological experiences.

"This dark comedy is not for the squeamish," she advises the reader. She isn't wrong.

I carry six-week-old Dagney around in the same brown, owl-print carrier that I used for my older daughters, who are now seven and five. This spacing was deliberate; I knew if I was going to make the leap and have a third child, I'd need large chunks of the day where it was just me and the baby.

After I drop the big kids off at school, I have six hours to walk the city with my newborn and listen to podcast episodes. I unravel the cord for my earbuds and stick them into my ears, blocking out the grating cacophony of downtown Vancouver construction. I wrap us up in my husband's rain jacket, which is big enough to zip around both of us. Dagney is a large misshapen lump against my torso.

With a leopard-print mask covering my mouth and nose, I buy a coffee and step out into the November downpour. I walk along our street toward the Seawall, avoiding others with the appropriate six feet of distance, dodging garbage and the ramshackle tents that have sprung up everywhere in the West End since the pandemic began.

When I had Quintana in 2013, I was afraid I'd never write again. I didn't think I'd be able to focus on anything, especially since the pregnancy itself seemed to leach creative cells from my brain with each passing day. Instead, I walked. I spent that first year with her strapped against me in the owl carrier, often in tandem with friends who were also new moms. I repeated this pattern with each baby, spending my postpartum days walking until my hamstrings coiled tightly and my feet ached, until my hips would click and throb.

I walked in all weather. In the short-term snow of February in Vancouver after Quintana was first born. During the summer heat wave of 2015, with three-day-old Tamsin, sipping iced coffee and wandering down Davie Street, losing myself among the rainbow-bedazzled Pride floats. I walked her for hours at night, too, during the months she had colic and screamed at every street corner. Sometimes I'd strap her into the carrier and march her in loops around my apartment at midnight, trying to force sleep into her tiny but fierce lungs.

I listened to hours of podcasts. With Quintana, I listened to *The Longest Shortest Time*, a podcast about birth and new motherhood. With Tamsin, I became obsessed with *Terrible, Thanks for Asking*, a podcast that focused on horrific life experiences, usually illness, death, or some kind of trauma. Now, with Dagney, I listen to *You're Wrong About*, a podcast that analyzes people or events in the nineties that the public has misunderstood. I gravitate to the episodes that focus on the dark underbelly of motherhood. Grotesquely fascinating stories like "The Prom Mom," about a teenager who gives birth in a bathroom stall at prom and then disposes of the infant in the trash, or "Crack Babies," an episode that explores what the podcast's host describes as the "long history of white anxiety over black motherhood," mothers who were stigmatized and criminalized, their babies removed from their care and then neglected by the state.

While I wasn't writing, postpartum quickly became an incubation period for my work, and listening to podcasts helped my reeling brain snap into focus. Podcasts and walking with a newborn against my chest became a form of meditation, an opportunity to conceive and conceptualize poems and essays, a chance to spawn new ideas for the next project. I wasn't writing a single word during those early postpartum months, but podcasts kept me feeling like a writer. Examining and processing pregnancy and birth made me feel alive, as though I was massaging the very substance of humanity with my fingers.

By the time I arrive home from Stanley Park, I'm exhausted. While I try not to have specific expectations of how labour will go, it isn't going great. Even before the acupuncture, I was having contractions, and I haven't slept well in weeks. I anticipate being in labour most of the night but hope that by the time I'm ready to push, she'll slide out of me faster than the other two.

After my daughters are in bed, I spend the next few hours in the cocoon of my bedroom, the only light coming from the glow of my husband's cellphone as he reads articles to me in between contractions. As each contraction subsides, I immediately feel an intense pressure on my bladder, and stumble into the bathroom to release a trickle of pee. Then I return to the bedroom and bury my face in a pillow, waiting for the next one.

My doula arrives around midnight and sets up the TENS machine, a portable device with small vibrating patches that stick to my back. The patches transmit electrical pulses through my skin, spreading the harsh lightning bolt of pain from my contracting uterus, dulling it into a semi-manageable flame. The midwives are called and they arrive somewhere in the blur of labour.

I feel the urge to push with each contraction at this point, but the baby's positioning seems to be off. Birth is the ultimate metaphor for life; everything has to line up in order for a smooth experience. I bear down, feel my face tighten into a flushed grimace. Each push is a tree trunk ramming my tailbone from the inside.

There's no movement. No head barrelling down, no uterine muscles taking over. This baby is stuck. We are stuck. Pandemic stuck. Wildfire stuck. There's a body inside me that can't get out.

What seems to offend the reviewer of *Q & A* the most are the lengths to which I go to describe my body during birth.

"For Gruber, there is no distance, immersed as she is in her own maternity, drowning in bodily fluids."

In my earlier poetry collections, I wrote about my body extensively, exploring my sexuality, but once I experienced what it was like to grow a human and expel it, that interest became an avalanche of my own physiology. I felt a primordial intimacy with my body. Every part of me seemed to leak: In the third trimester, night sweats left my sheets soaked; postpartum lochia, or vaginal discharge containing blood, mucus, and uterine tissue continued for weeks after giving birth, while breast milk blotches darkened the front of all my shirts. After having kids, bodily functions quickly became a kind of muse. My literary bread and butter.

It's not just the fluids that inspired me to write about my body in this amount of detail. Pregnancy gave me no choice but to sit with a body that I had no control over. Each trimester came with its own burden—extreme nausea and fatigue, followed by fast weight gain and the futile search for clothes that fit gently around an expanding frame. There was the inability to walk more than a block during those last lingering weeks, my hips and back aching with every twist of position.

The murky weeks after birth are a strange alchemy all on their own. In the early weeks, you are overwhelmed with oxytocin, the "love hormone" that floods your body after birth to ensure bonding, but also cloudy from lack of sleep. There is only feeding your baby and leaking fluids. There is nothing to do but feed or juggle or rock this new, small body that you have made from your own.

I continue to push. The phase of moving a baby through the birth canal, coined as the "second stage," continues for hours, an anomaly for a third birth. I push in every conceivable position. Crouched on all fours with my face buried in a pillow. Lying on my side with one leg raised and extended. Slumped on the toilet, half asleep, blood sticky against my thighs. And finally, after three hours of this, in a squatting position with my belly thrust outward, my husband supporting me under my armpits as I scream and growl and catapult her out of me.

There are photos of these positions that I look at later. I am naked, as I always am in labour, my body running several degrees warmer than usual. Everyone else was freezing, but my skin stayed feverish to the touch, my frenzied body an exploding inferno.

"I have been on Adrienne Gruber's journey and it was not a bad experience, nor one I wish to forget," the reviewer of *Q & A* admits. "But I do not want to relive it through two dozen poems about someone else's milk and sweat."

While I am rereading this passage, Dagney naps and I eat Tamsin's leftover "flat eggs" (what she calls fried eggs) that have gone cold from sitting out all morning. I marvel at their saltiness; she added the salt herself. The eggs are a typical allegory of a life with kids, abandoned in the chaos and rush to get to school on time.

As a writer, this is what I have the time and energy to notice: the rubbery texture of the eggs, the slight sting of salt on my tongue. I can't articulate myself after a night of trying to keep my newborn asleep, but I can immerse myself in the sensory brine of a forgotten egg. In postpartum, I notice things otherwise unnoticed and I write about those things. Sometimes it's leftover gummy eggs; sometimes it's my own milk and sweat. Sometimes it's the moment Dagney wakes up, and I brush my lips against her cheek, notice how her skin is soft as butter.

"So, who should read the poems, if not other mothers?" the reviewer questions. "Would a woman who is not yet a mother be encouraged to put herself through a similar ordeal? Perhaps one or two of the poems are for men. Does their gathering into a one-topic volume make them another instance of separation from 'human experience?'"

When Teva Harrison's graphic memoir *In-Between Days: A Memoir About Living with Cancer* was published in 2016, I knew I needed to read it. Not because I could relate to her experience of living with metastatic breast cancer, but because I wanted to know what this very specific, very personal experience was like or at least, what it was like for her. What I know of how cancer ravages the body is only from reading gritty memoirs like Harrison's, from being fortunate enough to be a witness to this complex and brutal world.

At the Vancouver launch of *Q & A*, I invited two cis male poets to read with me. Both of them had written about becoming fathers. I was recently invited to write a blurb for a writer whose upcoming book of poetry is about his husband and his own experience of welcoming their son into the world via a surrogate. I follow trans men on Instagram who've carried and birthed babies, under the hashtag #seahorsedad, a nod to the male seahorse who gestates the eggs in his pouch. Birth and pregnancy are not limited to the experiences of cis women; there is room for everyone in the conversation.

I don't write about birth and parenting in the hopes that others will be encouraged to seek experiences that I've had. I don't know a single writer who does this. I write about my experiences because having kids broke me open in a way that nothing else has, and for a writer, that's a gift. I've never been as fascinated or reckoned with a process in the way I have with birth.

I have never felt so close to death, and so grateful for my own survival.

Toward the end of her analysis of my book, the reviewer casually mentions that she herself has four children. According to her website, she is in her early eighties, and because of that it is likely that my births looked a great deal different from hers. I'm not sure what her experiences were, but when she gave birth, fathers weren't allowed in delivery rooms and home births, once common, had become rare. Obstetricians transitioned birth to hospitals and midwifery was illegal. There were few options for women who wanted agency and autonomy in their births.

I wonder if lingering first-wave feminism drew her to my book, but also kept her from identifying with it. After all, twilight sleep was championed in the first half of the twentieth century by white feminists, many of whom considered it wildly misogynistic for women to be deprived of pain medication during childbirth: a societal norm, in part, due to the popular Biblical rhetoric that the pain of childbirth was God's punishment to women for Eve's great sin. Women who opted for twilight sleep woke up after giving birth with no memory of the experience. They were handed a swaddled newborn and left with the sense that they had been in control of their birth, that it was painless, and therefore empowering. Only, as it turned out, it wasn't painless. Women experienced all the pain and grotesqueness of birth, but the combination of drugs meant that they didn't remember a thing.

Twilight sleep also meant they had to be restrained, sometimes suited up in straitjackets and tied to their beds so they wouldn't lash out from pain and attack the nurses and doctors, or themselves. Women were often left in padded cages, eye masks used to block out the light and cotton balls stuffed into their ears so they wouldn't hear their own screams. It turned out that feminists weren't fighting for painless childbirth; they were fighting to forget childbirth, and the pain that goes along with it.

At first, doctors resisted the movement, but as it caught on it became easier to simply drug women and restrict access to the delivery room. Rather than providing women with more control over their birth choices, twilight sleep robbed them of their agency.

While this era of medicating women to the point of erasing their memory is long over, there still seems to be a lack of full disclosure when it comes to birth. Another poet who reviewed *Q & A* had a unique take as a woman who has never given birth and does not have children: "This is not the airbrushed and photoshopped recollection of childbirth that we hear about after women have given birth," she writes. "In my experience, too many women friends seem to have had really wonderful birthing experiences. Have they told me the truth, or is there a secret society of women who promise they won't tell honest stories of birthing?"

I've had three home births that went, by all accounts, as smoothly as one could hope, with few interventions and no medical issues. My body recovered well, and I ended up with a healthy baby every time. But each one of my births was strikingly different, both emotionally and physically. My expectations differed, and the way I processed each varied in its intensity. So maybe there is a secret society that hopes to be less secretive, that wants to reveal more than what the media offers. None of my experiences are out of the ordinary, but they aren't the Instagram worthy experiences we expect.

"What the poet does here, though, is peel back the superficial glow that is more socially presented and speaks instead—realistically—of how a woman's body can be nearly broken by the birth experience, and how her mind and body will be changed forever afterwards."

I don't think anyone is lying or telling euphoric birth stories as a cover-up. Rather, we haven't figured out how to talk or write about birth because it is not, and never has been, a straightforward experience. While often depicted in the media in extremes, either gruesome and horrific or blissful and euphoric, birth isn't the dichotomy it's portrayed to be. Perhaps that's why it's challenging, and even impossible, to sum up birth into a collective experience: each birth may share commonalities, but each story is wildly varied and unique.

My three daughters and I leave our apartment building one morning in October just weeks after Dagney is born. She is snuggled against my chest in the carrier, and Quintana and Tamsin trail behind me, cranky and sullen from being rushed out the door. We see a flattened squirrel on the concrete ahead, his legs stretched hopelessly. He's fallen from the ledge of our building several stories up and looks like Wile E. Coyote from *Looney Tunes*—still alive, but in shock.

As we approach, the squirrel is frantic, dragging his paralyzed legs and desperate to escape up a tree and away from us. My daughters beg to stay and help, but we have to get to school, so we leave him to fend for himself. It is callous of me, but I can't manage to care for another living thing.

I drag myself around with my kids, exhausted. Nights are not easy and mornings are even worse, as my husband and I struggle to get three kids dressed, fed, and out the door. I have to walk the older two to school, then walk the baby around the city so she naps.

I wonder when I'll write again, and if anyone will want to read about the small world I inhabit.

Just as the reviewer was wrong about my book, I was wrong about becoming a mother. I thought it would soften my brain and rob me of focus. Instead, motherhood gives me an infinite amount of material to work with and compels me to zero in on subject matter. It allows me to sink deeply into a topic without worrying about who is going to appreciate the finished product. Becoming a mother helps me to care much less about what others think.

After dropping the girls off at school, I walk Dagney around downtown, stopping at stores, a coffee shop for lunch. I listen to a new episode of *You're Wrong About*, where the podcast hosts debunk the diagnosis of Shaken Baby Syndrome. At some point, I check Instagram, and my building manager has posted a photo of the squirrel wrapped in an old blanket and tucked into a box. By the time she went outside to rescue it, it was already dead and crows were circling.

I tell Quintana and Tamsin what happened to the squirrel when I pick them up from school, that there was nothing to be done but have it buried before the crows picked it apart. They're fascinated by death these days, just as they were with birth in the weeks leading up to their sister's. They want to see where the squirrel is buried, place offerings of flowers and small stones at its grave, just as they wanted to see Dagney's slick head stretch and split me open like a bursting cosmos.

They want to witness it all.

NOTES

"Monsters" features a reference to an article by Tia Ghose, "Baby Born Pregnant with Her Own Twins," published February 10, 2015 (https// www.livescience.com/49766-baby-pregnant-twins.html). The quote from Michel Odent in "Monsters" was from the documentary, *The Business of Being Born*, directed by Abby Epstein and released in 2008 (Ricki Lake and Abby Epstein).

Information about the olfactory senses and the biochemical reaction of cut grass found in "The Smell of Screaming" comes from an article by Mara Grunbaum, "Why Freshly Cut Grass Smells Good," published May 5, 2019 (https://www.livescience.com/65400-why-freshly-cut-grass-smells-good.html).

"A Route That Does Not Include Your Child" contains direct quotes from the Gene Weingarten article "Fatal Distraction: Forgetting a Child in the Backseat of a Car Is a Horrifying Mistake. Is It a Crime?" published in the *Washington Post* on March 8, 2009 (https://www. washingtonpost.com/lifestyle/magazine/fatal-distraction-forgetting-a-child-in-thebackseat-of-a-car-is-a-horrifying-mistake-is-it-a-crime/2014/06/16/8ae0fe3a-f580-11e3-a3a5-42be35962a52_story. html), as well as information about vehicular hypothermia, the basal ganglia, and Forgotten Baby Syndrome.

The quotes from Roman Paska were taken from the *New York Times* article by Sarah Boxer "Pulling Strings: The Geppetto Effect" published January 17, 1998 (https://www.nytimes.com/1998/01/17/arts/pulling-strings-the-geppetto-effect.html).

Information on microchimerism in "Chimera" is from Carl Zimmer's article in the *New York Times* "A Pregnancy Souvenir: Cells That Are Not Your Own" published September 10, 2015 (https://www.nytimes.com/2015/09/15/science/a-pregnancy-souvenir-cells-that-are-not-your-own.html).

Information about the Dutch famine and epigenetics discussed in "Vigil for the Vigilant" is from Benedict Carey's article in the *New York Times* "Can We Really Inherit Trauma?" published December 10, 2018 (https://www.nytimes.com/2018/12/10/health/mind-epigenetics-genes.html).

Quotes in "You're Wrong About" were taken from Phyllis Parham Reeve's review of *Q & A* in *BC Book Look*, published on January 5, 2021 (https://bcbooklook.com/568-pregnant-lines-and-pauses/) and Kim Fahner's review of *Q & A* in *periodicities: a journal of poetry and poetics*, published June 27, 2019 (https://periodicityjournal.blogspot.com/2021/01/kim-fahner-q-by-adrienne-gruber.html).

ACKNOWLEDGEMENTS

It's difficult to fully express my gratitude to all the people and organizations who have supported me throughout the last five years that I worked on this book. A book is never written in a vacuum. Here goes.

Thank you to:

The editors that published earlier versions of these essays and the contest judges who selected essays to be short-listed and/or placed. "Chimera" appeared in *The Fiddlehead*, "A Route That Does Not Include Your Child" in *SubTerrain*, "The Smell of Screaming" in *Pulp Fiction*, "Monsters" in *Event*, "Hunger: Notes to My Middle Daughter" in *Grain*, and "Fractal" in the anthology, *Don't Tell: Family Secrets*, published by Demeter Press.

The Canada Council for the Arts and the BC Arts Council, both of whom provided essential funding while I worked on this book.

The entire Book*hug team, especially Jay and Hazel. Your kindness, your support, and your belief in my work has carried me through many doubtful days. Thank you for understanding the vision for this book before I did.

My editor, Stacey May. Your careful and considerate reading of this book (multiple times!) was such a gift. Thank you for your constant encouragement and for getting exactly what I was trying to say.

My CNF workshopping group. You've read pretty much every word in this book and kept me moving forward in the process. I'm in your debt.

My teaching colleagues, who have held me up professionally, and who have been nothing but supportive of my writing.

My parents, extended family, and friends, especially Anita, Emma, Mandy, Morgan, Taran, Linda, Matthew, Taunya, Mike, Amanda, and Richard.

Amy and Liz, for lifting this book up with your words.

"Chimera" is for Liz, who showed me that it's possible to be a writer, teacher, and mom of three and not completely lose myself.

"Monsters" is for Brecken, who knows and loves the monster in me.

"You're Wrong About" is for Kim, who sees the gore in my writing as valuable and necessary.

"I Let Out My Breath" is for Jen, for holding your breath with me.

"The Smell of Screaming" is for Allison, who first told me about what happens to grass, and for always letting me scream as long and as loud as I need to.

"Erosion" is for my sister Edith, who truly understands the legacy we're inheriting, and who is completely irreplaceable.

"Martyrs" is for Bev, who knows what it takes to mother, and gives all her best energy to my girls.

"Vigil for the Vigilant" is for my husband, Dennis. You let me put you in these pages, even when it makes you uncomfortable. You let me write the stories I need to write about our life together, even when my lens is skewed in my own favour. You are unbelievably kind, and I'm the luckiest to have you.

"Fractal" is for Quintana, "Hunger: Notes to My Middle Daughter" is for Tamsin, and "Blood Month" is for Dagney. Each of you broke me open in your own way. I often fall short at being the mom you deserve, but at the end of the day the three of you are eager to love me as I am. That's a gift I won't ever take for granted.

ABOUT THE AUTHOR

©Quintana Roo Gruber-Hill

ADRIENNE GRUBER is an award-winning writer originally from Saskatoon. She is the author of the poetry collections *Q & A*, *Buoyancy Control*, and *This Is the Nightmare*. Both her poetry and non-fiction has been longlisted for the CBC Literary Awards. Adrienne lives with her partner and their three daughters on Nex̱wlélex̱m (Bowen Island), the traditional territory of the Coast Salish peoples.

COLOPHON

Manufactured as the first edition of
Monsters, Martyrs, and Marionettes: Essays on Motherhood
in the spring of 2024 by Book*hug Press

Edited for the press by Stacey May Fowles
Copy edited by Shannon Whibbs
Proofread by Laurie Siblock
Type + design by Tree Abraham

Printed in Canada

bookhugpress.ca